inside→out Worship

MATT REDMAN
AND FRIENDS

survivor

First published in the UK by Survivor 2005

ISBN 1-84291-226-7

Survivor is an imprint of Kingsway Communications Ltd,
Lottbridge Drove, Eastbourne BN23 6NT

Printed in the USA

Reproduced by arrangement with Regal Books, USA.

Searching the Psalms

 Taking it forward

 Theology of Worship

 A grounded life

 Insights

CONTENTS

INTRODUCTION

Welcome to *Inside-Out Worship*—the second volume in the *Heart of Worship Files* series. I hope this book will serve you in your quest to be ever more passionate and purposeful in the worship of God.

These are days to worship with both exuberance and understanding. So passion, yes. But purpose, too. We need to know where we're going in worship—and why we're going there. Explode with passion, yes; but explode purposefully, in the right direction. With so much excitement around the word "worship" right now, it's vital that we root ourselves in Bible-shaped practices and expressions. I hope this book, compiled from previous content on the heartofworship.com website, will help you on your journey.

Throughout the pages of *Inside-Out Worship*, we draw on the knowledge and experience of many leaders, scholars and lead worshippers from around the world. While some of the pieces in this book will be particularly relevant for pastors and worship music teams, I hope much of it will be a useful tool for anyone with a heart to probe deeper in worship.

The main teaching pieces in this book are divided into four sections:

Searching the Psalms

The Psalms themselves are songs of both passion and purpose. They inspire us and instruct us in our worship today. This section is a short series of devotional studies, searching back through these powerful ancient songs.

Taking It Forward

When it comes to leading gathered worship, there are certain skills, mind-sets and heart standards that are invaluable. In the "Taking It Forward" section, we look at these worship-leading essentials—practical and spiritual approaches that will help us keep moving on as lead worshippers.

Theology of Worship
Foundations are vital—they determine whether what we are building will stand or fall. It's vital that we build upon what God has revealed to us of Himself and His ways. This section helps us to lay God-centred and Scripture-shaped foundations in worship.

 A Grounded Life
This section is all about worship in the real world. Whether gathered together on a Sunday, or scattered all over town throughout the week, as the Church, it is essential that we work our worship through the whole of our lives. These articles present a challenge to ground our worship in the everyday reality of life.

Throughout this book you will also find "*Insights*"— a series of mini-teachings in which we glean guidance from some of today's most seasoned leaders and lead worshippers

I hope this book will fuel you in your life as an *inside-out* worshipper. May you be consumed with a love for God that burns so strongly on the inside that it cannot help but explode outward in passionate songs, sounds and service for God!

Matt Redman

INSIDE-OUT WORSHIP

DARLENE ZSCHECH

The best worship is inside-out worship. Worship is born from revelation. It's not outside in—something that simply looks good, has the band in place, the choir doing their thing and the church building looking beautiful. Our outside expressions may or may not involve these things, but the true test is always this: When we strip it all down, is there something of substance that is left?

The greatest worship is always inside out—devotion that flows from a changed life. Most of the great worship songs throughout history have been born from momentous occasions on the inside of a human being.

WORSHIP-LEADING ESSENTIALS

(Part 1) The Gentle Persuasion of Authority

MATT REDMAN

The "gentle persuasion of authority" is a mysterious thing. It overrides natural skill levels and defies formulas. It cannot be emulated or copied, and certainly not manufactured. It is a God-given anointing—a divine hand of favour upon a person that leads to spiritual successes in ministry. When a lead worshipper is entrusted with it, he or she effortlessly opens doors in worship meetings that might otherwise have remained shut. No force is required from the person ministering—the strength comes from God alone. Not by might, nor by power, but by His Holy Spirit.

The prophet Samuel told the newly anointed Saul, "Now do whatever your hand finds to do, for the Lord is with you" (1 Sam. 10:7). That is the gentle persuasion of authority. Saul did not need to fight for the crown of kingship, or manipulate his way to the throne. The hand of God was upon him, easing him into his destiny, and making otherwise impossible accomplishments fall naturally into place.

Those entrusted with the anointing of God achieve far more than logic says they should achieve. I know a few evangelists whose words bear fruit in a certain inexplicable way. Yes, they speak truth, as we all aim to—yet they also possess an uncanny knack of opening up God-conversations with those who don't know Him. It is not just a technique, nor is it just fantastic social skills or charisma, though it may employ these. It is more than just the sum of these natural gifts and personality traits. It is the gentle persuasion of the Holy Spirit's authority resting upon them. God has called them to a task and backs up this calling with a supernatural sense of favour.

One of the best examples of this gentle persuasion of authority in recent history is the ministry of Billy Graham. Countless numbers of people have gathered to hear the gospel message preached by this man, and multitudes have responded by giving their lives to Christ. But here is the mystery: in natural, earthly terms, perhaps there are even better speakers on the "circuit". Please don't misunderstand me—I love to hear Billy Graham preach—but the fruit of his ministry is far greater than the sum of his words. His impact does not come from shouting or ranting and raving all over the stage in a blast of energy. Nor does it come merely from persuasive and poetic words. It is an unforced accomplishment—the authority resting upon him gently persuades where other efforts would fail. He simply stays faithful and obedient to the calling on his life, and God backs up this incredible calling with a holy authority resting upon his life ministry.

So what does this mean for a lead worshipper? For one thing, we'll never need to "strut the stage" or "work the crowd", frantic to make something happen in worship time. We are not attempting to stir something up. Of course, we desperately want to see worship stirred up, but it is the Holy Spirit, and not us, who does the stirring. We need to adopt a posture of obedience and trust, and ease into the calling upon us. I've seen worship leaders who are amazing musicians, with mesmerizing skills, yet unable somehow to lead the people of God into the depths of congregational worship. Something is missing. It is the gentle persuasion of authority.

It's good to note at this point that there's nothing wrong with being passionate. We're not trying to be so laid back that we don't wholeheartedly throw ourselves into the worship. I once read a worship leader's article suggesting that it was wrong to sweat while leading worship. To the writer, this implied too much effort being put in and not enough dependence upon God. The heart standard of dependence is of course vital—but I'm not convinced it's inextricably linked with the glands under our armpits! Sweating more likely implies passion—and it's essential that we're passionate. The point is, whatever our outer posture is, our inner posture must be one of complete dependence. A knowledge deep down inside that the power of God upon us will always be the deciding factor. So be passionate, yes, but never fall into the trap of being forceful.

When God's hand of authority and anointing rests upon a person, it is a weighty entrustment. Anointing does not guarantee godly character; in fact it tests it to the extreme. Our character must be strong enough to handle the entrustment of God's anointing. When the gentle persuasion of authority rests upon our lives, we can become popular and even powerful within the circles in which we minister.

Anointing turns the heat up—and it becomes more essential than ever to ruthlessly and constantly check the motives of our hearts.

The Old Testament shows us that God can win a battle through a small shepherd boy with a sling, some stones and a staff in his hand—and He can also win the day through a huge army. The constant is the hand of God's authority upon them. At other times, we see the people of God losing the battle because God has withdrawn His hand of favour. In the same way, the best musicians and the biggest sound system around will never take the place of the anointing of God. There is no substitute for the hand of God. Practise your instrument hard, yes. Learn songs and build a great team, absolutely. These are all important elements to worship leading. But all the while we improve our skills and harness our gifts, we must humbly remember their place in the grand scheme of things. The bottom line is this: We win or lose the day dependent on the hand of God. His gentle persuasion of authority resting on our lives will always be the deciding factor.

PICTURES OF JESUS

DON WILLIAMS

Give us commanding and compelling pictures of our Lord Jesus Christ. Give us stories about Jesus—His preaching the Kingdom, His healing the sick, His delivering the demonized, His radical call to discipleship, His entering into people's suffering, His always telling the truth, His seeking the lost and the marginalized, His confrontations with His enemies, His matchless teaching.

Give us clear, wonderful, compelling pictures of Jesus to fill our minds and engage our hearts in real worship. I challenge you to write this into your worship songs. May we sing *to* Him and *about* Him as the only One who really lives, and who shows us how to live.

PSALM 119

Inseparable: The Essential Link Between Worship and Word

LOUIE GIGLIO

Recently, while speaking to a large group of young people, I had a temporary moment of insanity and challenged the audience to memorize an entire book of Scripture. At first people looked at me like I had lost my mind. But soon a sort of "group euphoria" overcame us and people began to think, *I can do this!*

Well, that was over a month ago and the initial wave of excitement has faded. I would guess only a few are still pressing ahead. But this past week one of those few fuelled my heart with renewed hope for the lead worshippers of the future. I noticed him with his laminated copy of Colossians and asked how he was doing. "I've memorized all of chapter 1 and am moving into chapter 2," he replied. And he's just the guitar player in the band, not even the "up front" worship leader! Wow! (I'm smiling.)

You see, worship and the Word are inseparable. As worshippers and lead worshippers, we must continually link our lives to the living Word of God, both to nourish our souls and to feed our flocks.

Contrary to modern culture, worship does not begin with music, but with God. In fact, everything begins with Him, the living *Logos* (Word), the Alpha and the Omega—Beginning and End. So we read in the opening of John's Gospel, "In the beginning was the Word, and the Word was with God, and the Word was God" (John 1:1). Announcing the arrival of Christ on Earth, John writes, "And the Word became flesh and dwelt among us" (v. 14, *NASB*).

If we believe Jesus is pre-eminent, and, therefore, must be the centrepiece of our living and our worship, a little common logic leads us down this path: Jesus is the centre of all true worship.

Jesus is the Word of God.

Therefore, the Word of God is the centre of all true worship for all time.

It has always been interesting to me that the longest chapter in Scripture, Psalm 119, is about the psalmist's love affair with God's Word. Right in the middle of this amazing handbook of praise, we find the "lead worshipper" celebrating the essential role of the Word in his own life. It's there we find the confession: "Seven times a day I praise you for your righteous laws" (Ps. 119:164). Notice the daily link between worship and the Word in David's life. All throughout the day, the psalmist was thanking God for the truth. Yes, he was always praising God. But he was also thinking about God's Word every minute of the day. That's why he goes on to say, "May my lips overflow with praise, for you teach me your decrees" (v. 171). If I'm reading this right, the source of the psalmist's worship is the activity of the Word of God in his life. In his case, the work of the Word preceded the "overflowing" of praise to God. If you're like me, you hear people praising God all the time. But when's the last time you were around people who were "overflowing" with worship because of the impact God's Word was making in their lives?

Songs alone don't change people. It's the truth that sets us free. As lead worshippers, it's essential that we immerse ourselves in His Word and allow His Word to reshape and contour our hearts. In fact, God only has one ultimate goal for us all—the goal of being conformed to the image of His Son (see Rom.

8:29). To be conformed is a tough and arduous task, a journey that leads us to the anvil and the altar, moment by moment. It's a process of transformation that results from consistently renewing our minds by God's truth (see Rom. 12:2).

If we're not careful, we can quickly inhale the feelings and emotion we experience in corporate worship, only to go away with little lasting and substantive change in our souls. In other words, we are prone to joyfully uttering the words of praise, while continually dodging the sword of the Spirit. As a result, our worship becomes a counterfeit shell while our hidden heart fails to embrace His truth for our lives.

If my gifted guitar-playing friend keeps plugging away in Colossians, he'll soon be encouraged by this challenge in chapter 3: "Let the Word of Christ dwell in you richly as you teach and admonish one another with all wisdom, AND as you sing psalms, hymns and spiritual songs with gratitude in your hearts to God" (Col. 3:16, emphasis added). What begins with a heart set on His Word will always end in a song of praise to our God.

So gently lay down the guitar and pick up the Word of God. Within its pages are life and breath—and everything.

REMEMBERING THE STORY

J. D. WALT

We need more songs that narrate the story of God—songs that cause us to remember the great saving acts of God in history. If you look through the Psalms, they are continually lifting up the imagery of Passover and Red Sea, of Sinai and Promised Land, of Exile and Return. The story of God is itself embedded in their worship.

We need to find better ways of doing this in our time—ways of explicitly embedding the story of God in our singing, which serves to make it more alive in our communal memory. Doing this will give rise to Kingdom imagination. For it is only in remembering the mysterious, unconventional and unpredictable ways of God that we imagine them in our time.

But first and foremost we remember the story

not for how it benefits us—though it does greatly enlarge our souls—but because it glorifies God.

WORSHIP-LEADING ESSENTIALS

(Part 2) The Awakening Power of Truth

MATT REDMAN

The truth of God has power to awaken us. Many times my heart has been slumbering—I've felt a certain numbness in my walk with God, and found myself lacking in energy and passion. Before too long I start looking for the reason. Overworked? Perhaps. Distracted? Perhaps. More often than not I realize I've fallen for the same old trick. I've been neglecting the Word of God—somehow trying to move on with God without the daily bread of Scripture. Often it takes just a single, piercing line of His truth to begin the wake-up call in my soul, whet my appetite and begin to brighten my walk with God. One passionate psalm, one wise proverb or a few words from the mouth of Jesus in the Gospels, and I know I've come to the right place. Before long, I'm worshipping.

Taking it to a congregational level, it's vital that our worship gatherings are full of truth.

Kevin Navarro comments, "Every worship leader must become a theologian."[1] As leaders involved in gathered worship, we're placed in a position of great responsibility. And to handle that entrustment well, we need to become students of the Word of God. This will lead us to choose God-honouring expressions of truth that ensure we're rallying around the essential focus points of our faith, and at the same time defend our services from misleading theology. It is said of the old preacher Charles Spurgeon, that "his blood ran bibline"—that if you'd have cut him, the Bible would have flowed out. What an amazing tribute! Oh, for worship songs and services that bleed with the Word of God! But if we want to bleed the Bible, we have to read the Bible. If we want to bleed the truth of God, we have to feed upon the truth of God.

Planning for congregational worship comes with much responsibility—for, like it or not, what we end up singing in our gatherings will, especially over time, affect people's view of God. Think, too, for a moment of the unchurched visitor—what you sing about (or don't sing about) in those few minutes can have a profound effect as these seekers are introduced to God. Marva J. Dawn comments that a worship service may never contain every single aspect of God's truth, but "worship must never give us untruth".[2]

It's also important that we make an effort to ensure that none of the major ingredients is missing. Over a decade ago, the Vineyard Movement was leading a conference in Australia. As a response to the content of the worship songs, one pastor wrote to John Wimber (who led the Vineyard Movement) and pointed out that out of around 70 songs in the conference songbook, only a few directly referenced the Cross.[3] His point being that the centrality of the Cross is essential in Christian worship. Wimber was grateful for this insight from an outsider, and shocked by it, too. He immediately set about feeding his songwriters once again on the beautiful truths of the Cross, sending many of them some of the major Christian writings on the Cross. Sure enough, many new songs flowed out, centring around the truth of the Cross. Out of the overflow of the heart, the mouth speaks (Matt. 12:34). The more we digest the revelation of Scripture, the more powerfully it will affect the way we write and choose worship songs.

The truth of God sets us free to worship. Many times I've witnessed a congregation resounding with a certain lyric—a powerful display of God's revelation in the line of a song, which resonates deeply in the hearts of those singing it. Perhaps a little moment where people let out a cheer of praise or some other sign of agreement as they receive a glorious truth of God. A good example is the hymn "Thine Be the Glory"—which powerfully presents the glorious truth of the resurrection of Jesus. Each time we arrive at the line, "Endless is the victory, Thou over death hast won!"[4] there is an upsurge in worship. Hearts all around the room are experiencing the awakening power of truth.

Too often, we mess around trying to make something happen in congregational worship times. And we underestimate the awakening power of God's truth. Worship, as John Piper described it, is meant to be a "glorious feast on the perfections of Christ".[5] Songs and services must present the glories of our Lord Jesus—and then provide appropriate ways to respond to this splendour. The healthiest congregational worship times give us space to both inhale and exhale; to breathe in the powerful revelation of God, and then breathe out with a cry of praise and devotion. The best worship songs poetically, relevantly and biblically capture the truths of God, and at the same time also give the worshipper a way of responding to these truths. A great example of this is Tim Hughes's song "Here I Am to Worship". The verses take us through the powerful truth of the incarnation of Jesus: "Light of the world you stepped down into darkness" and "Humbly you came to the earth you created, all for love's sake became poor". And the chorus gives us an opportunity to respond to that beautiful truth: "Here I am to worship, Here I am to bow down, Here I am to say that You're my God."[6]

The truth of God has power to wake up both the lost and the found. To bring fresh flame to fading embers, and to ignite for the first time a fire in the hearts of those who had never before seen Him. As leaders of worship, let us never underestimate the awakening power of God's truth.

CHOOSING SONGS

TODD PROCTOR

I plan worship sets that partner with the message being preached. At Rock Harbor Church, most of our worship is "backloaded", creating a path of response to the truth from God's Word. In preparing music, I try to choose a progression of songs that first linger in the revelation from Scripture, and ultimately lead to sacrifice.

One thing I have discovered in this process is the importance of "prepared spontaneity"—bringing many more songs than we will actually use. This allows us to adjust to the Spirit's move in the moment—especially with band and lyric projection team in tow. We have found great freedom in not being confined to a predetermined script, yet still having enough language to sustain intimate conversation with God. In choosing worship songs, I prayerfully anticipate several different directions the Holy Spirit could take this conversation, and try to "pack enough songs" to follow.

A grounded life

WHEN THE TEARS FALL . . .

TIM HUGHES

Have you ever sung this song in church?

> He has driven me away and made me walk
> in darkness rather than light; indeed, he
> has turned his hand against me again and
> again, all day long . . . He has broken my
> teeth with gravel; he has trampled me in
> the dust (Lam. 3:2-3,16).

Or what about this one?

> How long, O LORD? Will you forget me
> forever? How long will you hide your face
> from me? How long must I wrestle with
> my thoughts and every day have sorrow
> in my heart? (Ps. 13:1-2).

I'm guessing you probably haven't sung either of these. Most of the churches I've visited sing songs of celebration, joy, praise and adoration—which is wonderful—but seem to miss the songs of lament. They are deemed as inappropriate or melancholic. I remember hearing one worship leader say that each Sunday he only had 25 minutes to lead worship through song, so why would he want to waste time focusing on the negative?

In his article "The Hidden Hope in Lament", Dan Allender writes,

> Christians seldom sing in the minor key. We fear the somber; we seem to hold sorrow in low esteem. We seem predisposed to fear lament as a quick slide into doubt and despair; failing to see that doubt and despair are the dark soil that is necessary to grow confidence and joy.[1]

A quick glance through the Psalms and many other books in the Bible reveals so much pain and lament—cries of despair and suffering continually offered up to God. This begs the question: Have we lost the place for worship and lament in the Church?

A while back I wrote a song called "When the Tears Fall". It was written at a time when life for me was hard. I'd taken a few knocks and suddenly my heart was filled with questions and doubt. One evening, feeling very low, I sat down and started pouring out my heart to God. The first line I sang out was, "I've had questions without answers. I've known sorrow, I have known pain."[2] Immediately, I looked for a response. How do you follow a line like that? Well the answer is, look to Jesus. Everyone on this earth experiences pain, suffering, bereavement and illness. The only difference is that for those who believe that Jesus is Lord, we have a Saviour we can turn to and cling to.

> But there's one thing that I'll cling to;
> You are faithful, Jesus, You're true.[3]

As I sang out of my pain and doubt, my soul found rest in Jesus. At first I concluded this was a personal song only for my own use. However, the more I pondered it, I began to realize that the sentiment and theme of this song was just as worshipful as any other. For there has to be a place for pain in the Church.

We need a bigger picture of what worship is. Questioning God doesn't mean we are disobeying Him. Expressing doubt doesn't mean we are lacking faith. In our everyday living, the people we're most likely to share our deepest fears and questions with are those we most love and trust. It's an intimate thing to be honest and raw with someone. It's something that draws you closer to a friend. Expressing anger and pain in worship can actually be a beautiful, intimate thing. Again as Dan Allender says, "Lament cuts through insincerity, strips pretense, and reveals the raw nerve of trust that angrily approaches the throne of grace and then kneels in awed, robust wonder."[4]

If we return to the songs I quoted at the start, we see that they don't end where I left them. In Lamentations, the bitter cry ends with lines of hope and trust:

Yet this I call to mind and therefore I have hope: Because of the LORD's great love we are not consumed, for his compassions never fail. They are new every morning; great is your faithfulness (Lam. 3:21-23).

In the Psalms, the feeling of abandonment and sorrow is responded to by singing out,

> But I trust in your unfailing love; my heart
> rejoices in your salvation. I will sing to the
> LORD, for he has been good to me (Ps. 13:5-6).

It's easy to praise when everything is going according to plan. It's more of a challenge when everything around us is falling to pieces. It takes great faith to say, "You are good" when life is incredibly hard. But God is good and forever worthy of our praise. This is not dependent on our feelings. Day and night, always the same, God deserves our highest praise.

We will find great comfort and healing in the Church by allowing space to be honest and real about how we really feel. To allow questions and doubts to rise, but in that place to respond to God by worshipping His holy name.

> I will praise You. I will praise You.
> When the tears fall, still I will sing to You.
> I will praise You. Jesus praise You.
> Through the suffering still I will sing.[5]

WORSHIP AND SUFFERING

BETH REDMAN

When we think about worship, too often we think only about a joyful kind of noise. But at times, worship contains the sound of suffering. Wholesome worship sometimes means bringing songs and cries of pain to the God of grace.

In some seasons, life goes wonderfully. We're growing, dreaming and laughing. Suddenly a disappointment, discouragement or tragedy hits us so hard that we can barely take a breath. In our own personal lives, a few years ago, Matt and I excitedly awaited the birth of our son—only to see him, newly born, rushed down the corridor into intensive care, where his little life hung in the balance. Time for a different kind of worship song—what could we sing and say as we called on the name of God? Little Noah's breath was restored, and we felt the mercy and kindness of

God as he left the hospital healthy.

Time passed, and we were excited about being pregnant again. We entered the obstetrician's office for our first ultrasound scan. Moments later, our excitement turned to horror as we were calmly informed that our baby's heart was no longer beating.

A few days later, struggling to come to terms with this sadness and pain, I stumbled across a programme about "lightning" on the television. I was gripped by how awesome God is—realizing once again that whatever circumstances come my way, He continues to be the awesome, sovereign God—ever to be trusted, feared and adored. The Lord gives, and the Lord takes away. Wise worshippers live through every season with a cry of "Blessed be the name of the Lord" on their lips and in their hearts.

A grounded life

SPIRITUAL CONVERSATIONS OUTSIDE THE SANCTUARY

SALLY MORGENTHALER

I write this on a cold, snowy day in Denver, Colorado. After a glorious, unseasonably warm autumn, I can personally relate to Christina Rossetti's Christmas hymn: "In the bleak mid-winter, frosty wind made moan. Earth stood hard as iron, water like a stone."[1]

Actually, that hymn seems like a good starting place for what I have rumbling around in my head. Christina Rossetti wrote poetry and song lyrics 150 years ago. I'm interested by her use of that strange word, "bleak". Perhaps her world was more despairing than ours, and that's why she used it. But, considering the world events of the past few years, I doubt it. If anything, the "bleakness" factor seems to be going up, which makes the lack of songs relating to things bleak all the more glaring an omission. In a world where the haunting, postmodern lament "Bring Me to Life"[2] achieved worldwide, top-10 status for months in 2003, why is it so hard for us in the Church to sprinkle "bleak" into our worship repertoire? Perhaps Barry Taylor at Fuller Seminary is right: "The spiritual conversation is going on, but the church is not invited."[3]

Jesus knows all about bleak people and spiritual conversations that happen outside sanctuaries and worship spaces. In John 4, the Samaritan woman who approaches the well where Jesus was sitting was anything but ecstatic or "positive". (I'm not sure she would have done very well in most praise and worship settings.) She was alone and bereft. (Her first husband quite possibly had cast her aside for another woman.) No wonder she longed for the life this stranger said He could give—unending, unlimited, overflowing.

Jesus gave the woman at the well an incredible gift: the opportunity to bring her real self to a spiritual exchange. He gave her the chance to simply be who she was—sin, loneliness, doubts and all. Thus, in the privacy of her encounter with the Son of God, she was nurtured into naming her reality. And Jesus unflinchingly acknowledged that reality. He did not ask her to be happy, to adopt religious behaviours for the sake of image or to look in any way "together" when she clearly was not. No. Instead, He gave her the treasure of a completely honest relationship with herself and with God. Bottom line, Jesus knew who this woman was from the outset: a human being decimated in body and spirit. He knew she was a woman emptied of purpose, sapped of esteem—rejected and despised in a way that goes to the very epicentre of a woman's being. And He loved her in the midst of exactly who she had become.

Now, fast-forward two millennia. How intriguing that the first-century woman of John 4 and the postmodern woman in Evanescence's "Bring Me to Life" have such strikingly similar, image-peeling encounters with God. "Where I've become so numb without a soul, my spirit sleeping somewhere cold."[4] Now these are what I'd call "visceral" lyrics. They literally grab you from the inside. Can you imagine poetry this vivid in a worship song? You want bleak? That's bleak. Check out the digital backdrop created for the music video and you'll see bleak taken to yet another level.

Still, this is MTV, not church. You can get by with extremes in pop culture. People who watch that stuff expect dark. They expect to be shocked. The more realistic and edgy it is, the better. But it won't work for worship. Interesting. The psalmist David got by just fine with dark, edgy, bleak, real-life, cynical and downright ironic in some of his worship songs. And he wasn't writing for MTV. Check out what he had to say in Psalm 77:

> I yell out to my God, I yell with all my
>   might,
> I yell at the top of my lungs. He listens.
> I found myself in trouble and went looking
>   for my Lord;
> my life was an open wound that wouldn't
>   heal. . . .
> Will the Lord walk off and leave us for
>   good?
> Will he never smile again? (Ps. 77:1-2,7, *THE*
>   *MESSAGE*).

If David can write worship songs like this, dare we follow in his steps? T. S. Eliot has often been quoted as saying that Christians tend to make life neater and tidier than it really is. In reality, we live on an increasingly fractured planet, and, regardless of what we may have been taught, that fracturing encompasses the lives of Christian and non-Christian alike. Though Christ, by His blood, has forever opened to us the doors of heaven, we still live out our lives in the shadow of the Fall and are not, in the here and now, delivered from the temporal effects of it. (Perhaps this is what Jesus meant about experiencing tribulation.) Why is it, then, that our worship services so often mask the very tribulation Jesus acknowledged? Why do our songs and sermons become exercises in denial, rather than avenues to affirm the God at the centre of the hurricane? Somehow, if we just don't acknowledge the darkness—if we don't admit to addictions, fears, regrets, doubts, questions, confusion and disorientation—we think they don't exist.

Theologian and historian Walter Brueggemann has a cure for denial: lament. In his stunning foreword to Ann Weems's *Psalms of Lament*, Brueggemann unpacks the essence of biblical lament, offering not only an alternative view of Hebrew worship, but also a new and crucial window on the worship of the Early Church, which clearly adopted Hebrew psalmody—including lament—into its gatherings.

Nearly one half of the Psalms are songs of lament and poems of complaint. Something is known to be deeply amiss in Israel's life with God. And Israel is not at all reluctant to voice what is troubling (her). . . . The lament-complaint, perhaps Israel's most characteristic and vigorous mode of faith, introduces us to a "spirituality of protest." That is, Israel boldly recognizes that all is not right in the world. This is against our easy gentile way of denial, pretending in each other's presence and in the presence of God that "all is well," when it is not.[5]

Dare we imagine a genre of new millennial worship—songs that don't gloss over the doubts, the cynicism or our own humanity? Songs that refuse to minimize pain, but rather, lend voice to it? If we refuse this challenge, I fear that even our Gen-X evangelicalism will become uninhabitable by real people.

REMEMBERING THE POOR

Nigel Morris

We worship a God whose heart is for "the poor"—the socially marginalized and the downtrodden. When Jesus came, He came preaching good news to the poor. The ministry of Jesus has not changed. Through us, He is still preaching good news today.

The poor are not "those people"—they have names and faces, needs and desires, hopes and dreams—just like you and I. We are called to worship God with every part of life. One way of doing this is to express His heart and provision by touching real people with real needs.

Worship is incomplete without these expressions of compassion. "Remember the poor" is a cry that resonates throughout all of Scripture and must resound in our worship too.

WORSHIP-LEADING ESSENTIALS

(Part 3) The Shepherding Instincts of a Pastor

MATT REDMAN

I used to think I wasn't a pastor. Every now and again, different folk would suggest this role might be part of my calling, and every single time in my heart I'd say, *No, that's not me. I'm a worship leader ... a musician ... a songwriter. I'm no pastor.* I just didn't see myself as that sort of person. I was your introverted creative type, and if people wanted some pastoral support, they'd be better off talking to one of my highly sensitive pastor friends.

Then one day it dawned on me. Every lead worshipper has to be a pastor. In other words, every lead worshipper needs to care about people. To be leaders of the people of God in worship, we need to care deeply about those with whom we journey. I may never become a "Pastor" with a capital *P* and adopt the full title. But from the day I accepted the role of lead worshipper in my cell group, I became a pastor with a little *p*. In saying yes to leading the praises of God, I was also saying yes to pouring my heart into the people of God. The call to be a lead worshipper is, in part, the call to be a shepherd.

A heart for music alone is simply not enough. "But I'm just the keyboard player," you might protest. "All I need to do is press the right keys at the right time, and it'll all be cool." Not quite. A heart for music is one thing, and it's a good, God-given thing. But a heart for music must always be outweighed by a heart for the people. Otherwise we're in for a rough ride. I wonder if you've ever come across the electric guitarist type who, every now and again, launches into a four-minute solo during a worship song? Meanwhile the congregation look on confusedly, wondering if they will ever get to join in with this particular song again. What has happened here? Usually it's the same old thing—the "Clapton" in question has a great big heart for music, but a relatively small one for the people being led. I exaggerate to make a point—the message being that every member of the worship music team needs to seek God for a greater heart for His people.

At times in the past, I've come across a batch of fresh new songs from around the world and been desperate to use them all straight away. After all, they're fresh, they're original, and they're really helping me in my own walk with God. The musician in me is saying, *Go on, Matt—do them all this Sunday,* and my creative juices get flowing as I try to figure out how I could weave all five songs together into a seamless medley of fresh new tunes! But the pastor in me is giving some different advice: *Pace yourself, Matt. Pastor this new wave of freshness in. Try to ensure that every willing heart comes along for the journey. Allow people to feel at home, and always seek to balance the brand new with the familiar.*

Wisdom tells me that on the vast majority of these occasions, the musician in me must learn to submit to the pastor in me. People are more important than music. In worship meetings, music is a tool to help us all express our hearts to God, and to serve the people of God in such a pursuit. The people are never a tool to serve music. It's always the other way around.

As we develop pastoral hearts, we bring a whole new dimension to our worship leading. We see each other as a family, not just a Sunday morning club.

We look out as we lead and see a body of believers we care passionately about, and individuals with whom we share our lives. We give preference to one another in the worship team, weeping with those who weep, laughing with those who laugh, and spurring each other on to live a life of worship. Before we know it, there's a whole new depth to our worship leading. There's an authenticity that cannot be learned or rehearsed. Somehow the focus is no longer just to have a successful 20-minute "worship music slot" in our services. The focal point has become something much more meaningful—a burning desire to see the people of God move on to greater depths in Him.

A pastoral heart is not an optional extra, fitted only to "top-of-the-range" lead worshippers. It is a worship-leading essential.

RELATIONSHIP AND TEAM
BRIAN HOUSTON

As senior pastor of Hillsong Church, Australia, I am often asked about my relationship with our worship team. The greatest dynamic we have is probably our relationship and sense of team. It isn't a solo effort. Together we are building the Church of Jesus Christ, and we need each other to do it. The Word says that where there is unity, the Lord commands the blessing (see Ps. 133).

I am proud of our worship and creative arts team and rejoice at their opportunity. It isn't because of my leadership or even their gifts; it is the unity of spirit and commitment to the cause of Christ that has enabled our church to experience such a dynamic and blessed ministry. Insecurity can wreck a team. If I were insecure or threatened by the success of our worship team, I would probably suppress them, rather than release them to be raised up by God.

The commitment of the worship team to the health of our church is an important contribution to the equation of building a strong team. They have a sense of ownership because they are sons and daughters in God's house, not hirelings. Hirelings have their own agenda and use the church as an opportunity to build their own platform or go on to bigger and better things. By realizing that our church isn't a stepping-stone to somewhere else, or thinking that there is a better world out there, the key people on our worship team are committed to the church for the long haul.

UNDERSTANDING WORSHIP IN THE NEW TESTAMENT

(Part 1)

CHRIS JACK

In studying the practices and principles of Christian worship in the New Testament, the right starting point is surely the life and teaching of Jesus. The first significant thing to note is that Jesus Himself was a worshipper. Indeed, He is the one true worshipper. Yet, as David Peterson reminds us, He is more than just a model, or example:

> Jesus offers the perfect pattern or model of acceptable worship in his obedient lifestyle. Yet Jesus' life is more than an example of sacrificial service. His obedience proves to be the means by which the messianic salvation is achieved.[1]

As we study the theme of Jesus as a worshipper, there is a crucial fact of which we must remind ourselves—one that can all too easily be forgotten or ignored. Jesus was a Jew. Moreover, as the Gospel records amply demonstrate, He was a good Jew. This is nowhere more clearly reflected than in His approach to worship.

How did Jesus worship? What were His worship patterns? What did worship involve for Him? Jesus worshipped according to the established Jewish patterns and practices of His day. Let's review the main evidence:

- Jesus was circumcised, and presented to the Lord in the Temple (see Luke 2:21ff.).
- Jesus went to the Temple, as a boy, with His family (see Luke 2:41-42).
- Jesus regularly attended synagogues and taught there (see Matt. 4:23 [cf. Mark 1:39; Luke 4:15]; 9:35; 12:9ff. [cf. Mark 3:1ff.; Luke 6:6ff.]; 13:54ff. [cf. Mark 6:2ff.; Luke 4:16ff.]; Mark 1:21ff.; Luke 4:44; 13:10ff.; John 6:59; 18:20).
- Jesus prayed, and taught others to do so (see Luke 11:1ff.).

- Jesus fasted and taught others to do so (see Matt. 4:1-2; 6:16-18).
- Jesus blessed God for food (see Matt. 14:19 [cf. Mark 6:41; Luke 9:16]; Mark 8:7; Matt. 26:26 [cf. Mark 14:22; Luke 24:30]).
- Jesus taught others to observe the ceremonial requirements of the Law (Matt. 8:4 [cf. Mark 1:44; Luke 5:14]).
- Jesus referred to the Temple as "my Father's house" (Luke 2:49).
- Jesus was concerned for the purity of the Temple (see John 2:13-17; cf. Matt. 21:12-13; Mark 11:15-17; Luke 19:45-46).
- Jesus was willing to pay the Temple tax, albeit to avoid giving unnecessary offence (see Matt. 17:24-27).
- Jesus celebrated the main Jewish festivals: Passover (see John 2:13ff.; Luke 2:7ff. [cf. Matt. 26:17ff.; Mark 14:12ff.); Tabernacles (see John 7:2ff.); Dedication (see John 10:22ff.).
- Jesus lived a life of perfect submission and obedience to the Father (see Matt. 26:39 [cf. Mark 14:35-36; Luke 22:42]; John 4:34; 5:19, 30; 17:4).

Ralph Martin rightly speaks of Jesus as "One who honoured all that was best in the tradition of the ancestral faith and forms of worship".[2] Arthur Patzia comes to a similar conclusion: "For the most part, Jesus honoured the traditions of his faith and participated in religious life with his family and disciples."[3]

While Jesus, as a good Jew, upheld the Law and its requirements, not least in the area of worship, and while He Himself was a model worshipper, He followed in the tradition of the Old Testament prophets, in the form of stinging attacks against hypocrisy and formalism. There is no room here for mere ritualism, for religious observance devoid of heart reality (see Matt. 6:1-6,16-18; Mark 7:1-23 [see also Matt. 15:1-20; cf. Luke 11:37-41]; Matt. 23:1ff. (see also Mark 12:38-40; Luke 20:45-47).

Furthermore, although Jesus kept the Law He was at times radical in His interpretation of it. See, for example, the Sermon on the Mount (see Matt. 5–7). This radical approach is further evidenced in His attitude toward the Sabbath (see Matt. 12:1-8 [cf. Mark 2:23-28; Luke 6:1-5]; Matt. 12:9-14 [cf. Mark 3:1-6; Luke 6:6-11]; Luke 13:10-17; 14:1-6; John 5:1-18, cf. 7:21-23; 9:1-16). This issue lay at the heart of many of the disputes Jesus engaged in with the Pharisees and teachers of the Law. In all of this, Jesus consistently displayed a concern for the heart of worship as the right response to God and His commands—not merely the legalistic observance of external forms or rituals.

Did Jesus ever offer Temple sacrifice? That is an interesting question, the answer to which can be no more than speculation. While there is certainly no explicit statement in the Gospels to the effect that He did, neither is there any assertion that He did not. A case can be made either way. As it is, nothing hangs on it. And we simply don't know. What is clear is that Jesus finally rendered the whole sacrificial system obsolete by the once-for-all offering of Himself as the perfect sacrifice. This is, of course, one of the central themes of the book of Hebrews (see Heb. 10:1-18).

In Jesus, the Temple and its worship are superseded. This truth is reflected in Jesus' own teaching: in His assertion of being greater than the Temple (see Matt. 12:6) and in His comment about rebuilding the Temple (see John 2:19-22). Jesus actually fulfils the hopes and expectations of the Old Testament. All that the Jews of His day anticipated in the messianic era finds its true embodiment in Jesus.

Jesus did not come to destroy Judaism, but to bring it to its destined end in the worship of the new age.[4]

It is evident that although Jesus lived and worshipped within His Jewish context, he was not bound by it. For He pointed beyond it. Through Him, something new was about to happen. Yet this new thing was continuous with the old and sprang directly out of it. Jesus was and is the bridge between the old and the new. He fulfils the old by His perfect obedience to it, and in doing so, ushers in the new. Here, then, is the sense in which Jesus is more than just a model worshipper. As the ultimate sacrifice for sin (see Heb. 9:26,28; cf. Mark 10:45), Jesus becomes the means of worship, the One through whom worship is to be offered (see Heb. 10:19-22; cf. John 14:6). Jesus not only worships truly; He also makes true worship possible.

WORSHIPPING THE TRINITY

CHRIS COCKSWORTH

I long to hear our songs of worship get closer to the song of the Spirit, in which Jesus worships His Father. I love Jesus; the Spirit loves Jesus; the Father loves Jesus; and our songs must truly praise Jesus, give Him glory, honour Him as God and acclaim Him as Lord. In this, I know, the Father is glorified. And yet, sometimes, I feel that our worship songs do not allow the song that Jesus sings to the Father to be sung in me. Although the songs take me to Jesus, they don't always take me in, with, and through Jesus to the one He calls Abba. Put simply, I would love us to have more songs that take us to the Father. More technically, we need the Trinitarian geography of Christian worship to be made clearer in our songs of worship.

MAKING OUR WORSHIP MORE TRINITARIAN

Robin Parry

Christianity is God-centred, and God is the Trinity. So it follows that Christianity must be Trinity-centred. The same must be said about our worship and prayer. Worship is God-centred, and because God is the Trinity, our prayer and worship should be Trinity-centred. Worship is the face-to-face encounter of the Church with God—with Father, Son and Holy Spirit.

So central is the Trinity that every other Christian belief connects to it. The Trinity is the hub of the wheel called Christianity, in which all its spokes connect. Every aspect of Christian belief has the Trinity at the centre: the creation of the world and everything in it; humanity in the image of (the triune) God; the providence of God; God's redemption of the world through Christ (incarnation, ministry, cross, resurrection, ascension); the future of the world; the mission of the Church; prayer; worship; the Kingdom of God. Consider the following:

Creation. The Father created the universe through His Son by the Spirit's life-giving power. The universe began its existence and continues to exist by the work of the Trinity.

Redemption. The Father so loved the world that He sent His Son, conceived in Mary by the Spirit. The Son spoke His Father's words and did His Father's deeds all in the Spirit's power. On the cross, the Son offered His life to the Father through the Spirit. Three days later, the Father raised His Son through the Spirit and exalted Him to His right hand. From there the Father gave Him the Spirit to pour out on the Church.

Consummation. The Spirit will raise the dead, and the Son will judge everyone on behalf of His Father. All Christ's enemies will be placed under His feet, and then He will hand everything over to the Father so that God will be all in all.

The story of the Bible is God's story, and it is the story of the Trinity. Every act of God is an act of the three Persons working in unity. The same can be said for our own Christian lives and experience. We see it in the following.

Conversion. The Father sends his Spirit to convict people of their sin and of the truth of the gospel. The Spirit draws us to faith in Christ, and through Christ, to the Father. We are baptized into Christ in the Spirit and baptized in water in the threefold name of Father, Son and Holy Spirit.

Worship and Prayer. Acceptable worship and prayer is only possible because of the new and living way opened up by Jesus; and we can only go that way as the Spirit enables us. Worship is a "gifted" (given to us) response.

Mission. The Spirit enables the Church to join with Christ in His mission to the world on behalf of the Father. That is what mission is.

Going back to public worship, I have a strong suspicion that worship does more to shape the spirituality of Christians than just about anything else. There may or may not be formal teaching of a particular topic, but we learn by means of a kind of osmosis— just as we learn language. This makes public worship crucial in the spiritual formation of the Church. It is here that people will learn how to relate to the Trinity. It is here that the richness of the creating and saving deeds of the Trinity will come to expression. It is here that we will discover how to approach God through the Son and in the Spirit. It is in this forum that we will join together in honouring the Father, the Son and the Holy Spirit.

Can we really blame people for not seeing the relevance of the Trinity if we have stripped it from our songs and prayers? Expressing good theology in songs and services is not about dotting the *i*'s and crossing the *t*'s but about enabling people to worship and experience the true God more adequately.

So here are some final questions.

1. How can we learn to pray in ways that are more overtly Trinitarian?
2. How should songwriters change what they do to be more Trinitarian?
3. How can we select songs that, while not being overtly Trinitarian, can work together to bring the three Persons of God into our awareness?
4. Can the Lord's Supper/Eucharist be used to generate an awareness of the whole Trinity?

5. How can preaching be more Trinitarian?
6. Can we learn to see the Persons of the Trinity more clearly in the Bible reading we do?
7. How can the creative arts (painting, sculpture, dance, music, etc.) be used to foster a Trinitarian spirituality in worship?

All this really boils down to one question: How can we shape our public worship so that it facilitates a rich encounter with the Christian God? In an ideal model, our worship will ceaselessly and effortlessly move back and forth between the threeness of God and the unity of God. It will shift focus from Father, to Son, to Spirit and back again in a restless celebration of divine love and mystery. It will also highlight the deep relations within the Godhead by not allowing the worshippers to lose sight of any of the Persons. At times the worship will draw the Father into focus; however, the Son and Spirit will be there, out of focus, but still in our field of awareness. Other times the Son will attract our attention, but not in such a way that we do not see Father and Spirit. When the Spirit attracts our worshipping attention it will always be as the Spirit of the Father and the Spirit of the Son.

Worship that makes us aware of the interrelationships within the Godhead is fully Trinitarian worship. Trinitarian worship is always "through the Son" and "in the Spirit"—yet is woven from an ever-changing mosaic of songs, prayers, Bible readings, testimonies, Spirit-gifts, sermons, Holy Communion, drama, dance, art, and more. The variety is endless and the possibilities infinite. But at the heart of it all stands the mystery of the Holy Trinity.

WORSHIP AND COMMUNITY

DAVID RUIS

Pastoring is not just about running a church meeting, it is about leading a community on a journey of discovering God together. The Sunday meeting is when worship becomes part of that community's "faith language"—through the good and the bad, the ups and the downs, the times of joy and the times of discouragement, the times of clarity and the times of struggle.

I am dreaming for communities of faith to go on a "journey" together instead of being satisfied to just pull off good meetings. Then out of that sense of pilgrimage they can express a worship that's anchored to the history of faith, as well as unlock creative sounds and rhythms that express the present and future journey.

WORSHIP-LEADING ESSENTIALS

(Part 4) The Adventurous Pursuit of Creativity

MATT REDMAN

We worship the God of all creation. Everywhere we look, from the tiniest atom to the grandest galaxy, we find evidence of an extravagant and exuberant Creator God. Scientists and artists alike marvel at the dazzling design of creation. Whether we peer through a microscope at the detailed design of a butterfly wing or through a telescope at the star-filled canvas of a night sky, we find the stamp of the Creator's artistry.

We human beings are made in such a way that our ears can hear around 300,000 different tones, and our eyes distinguish between 8 million colour differences.[1] God has designed us to recognize and value His astounding creativity.

More than that, He has formed us to be creative ourselves. As worshippers of the Creator God, and as those made in His image, one of the best ways we express what's going on inside is through outward displays of creativity.

Creativity is essential when it comes to our congregational worship. It's a sign of abundant life. A healthy church will burst with new songs, new sounds and new sights. These things are explosions of the heart—the evidence of souls so caught up in the glories of God that they continually respond in imaginative and artistic ways. Creativity in its purest form is a reflex—a flash of inspiration coming forth from the artist who has glimpsed the splendour of the divine. Putting that into the context of a church worship service, creativity does not come from a desire to be musically clever, or to do something new just because variety, as we say, is the spice of life. Instead, it's an imaginative and heartfelt response to the received revelation of God. As we see more and more of the goodness, greatness and majesty of God, we find ourselves responding ever more imaginatively with creative expressions of joy, thanksgiving and reverence.

As well as being a response to God, creativity is also a reflection of Him. God reveals and expresses Himself creatively, and we find ourselves responding in a creative way. Yet as we do so, we also reflect Him to those around us. Creation voices a song of His glory:

> The heavens declare the glory of God; the skies proclaim the work of his hands (Ps. 19:1).

In the same way, our artistic expressions—through songs, sounds and sights—are to be reflections of Him. Of course, they will always be just the faintest whisper—subtle echoes of His true worth—and yet they play an important part in our proclamation of God.

I recently travelled to Australia for the annual Hillsong worship conference, and I encountered one of the most creative congregational worship expressions I have ever seen. The band brought innovative and interesting musical arrangements to the fresh worship songs. But it went far beyond the music. There was colour everywhere—lighting and visuals all conceived in an original and tasteful way. There was movement everywhere, too—teams of dancers and more than 100 singers, who at times all moved in unison. Most visually stunning of all were the huge pyrotechnics, which lit up the whole place at appropriate moments during the worship songs. In a sense, it was a display of the Lord's splendour—a call to worship—reminding us of the wonders of our God. It was a banner held high, to the lost and to the found, which spoke of the greatness of the God we were worshipping.

Now obviously we don't get a chance to create this sort of display every time we gather to worship. And yet, why in the Church do we so often see a lack of creative expression? As worshippers and lead worshippers of the Living God, we are called to the adventurous pursuit of creativity. If we're adventurous, creativity is possible even on the tightest of budgets.

In times past, the Church has stood on the cutting edge, leading the way in many forms of art and music within society. Looking through history we find that many of the great artists and poets were simply giving creative expression to their walk before God—and at the same time shaping culture. A few hundred years ago in England, many looked to the Church to lead the way through music—as they saw that the "ecclesiastical style" was the most pioneering and exciting sound around. And we must pray for the same in this day and age, for the arts are fantastic pointers to the glory of God. It's time to become more adventurous in our pursuit of creativity in worship.

Creativity is a mind-set that needs to be actively developed—especially if we have fallen into the "this is the way we do things" trap. It can start with the simple things. Paintings, projections and backdrops that, rather than remaining the same for months upon end, change regularly. Songs arranged in different ways, using a variety of instruments. Using various sizes of vocal groups. Even these simple things can be helpful ways of unlocking freshness in our time of worshipping through music.

One of the reasons we encounter a lack of creativity in the Church is that we have not created the right environment for it. Creative expression thrives under certain conditions and dies under others. In an environment of harsh criticism, and no room for artistic experimentation or risk-taking, the creative flow will soon perish. Yet, too often in the Church, we live under these conditions and all too quickly clamp down on any new forms of expression. Of course, creative types must learn to submit to authority and to love the people of God in such a way that they will always seek to bring in new expressions humbly and pastorally. But we must leave space to experiment, and room to grow in the arts.

In the worst-case scenarios, the blunt and practical tendencies of a pastor clash with the sensitive and reactionary personality type of an artist, and creative expression is soon wrapped in a straitjacket. In truth, the world often uses the arts as rebellion, and pastors are rightly concerned that this tendency does not creep into the Church. Yet, it is time to redeem the stolen goods—for the very best use of creativity is to praise and proclaim the Living God. We must make room for our artists to lead us in this. If you can't be creative in the Church, where can you be creative? Where the Creator is worshipped, and freedom abounds beneath the wonder of Calvary, surely there should be a momentous explosion of worshipful creativity!

One word of caution: Creativity is not always about new and innovative expressions. It can be equally powerful to re-present something old and redefine it as new. It could be a particular song or sound—or any art form from our church heritage. As the biblical saying goes, there is nothing new under the sun. Old things should therefore be celebrated and regenerated. Introducing a 500-year-old hymn may be just as creative as introducing a 5-day-old song. Both can be an expression of creativity, and both can unlock freshness in our congregational worship.

The worshipping church should be leading the way in all things creative. In the Church, we have more to sing about than the rest of this world. We have more reason to celebrate, more inspiration to dance and more grounds for all kinds of artistic expression. We have seen the glory of the One and Only—a revelation that should surely lead to explosive and imaginative heart responses.

And there is one final reason why the Church of God should be the standard bearer for creativity. We are those in whom the Holy Spirit lives, and He will inspire and equip us to respond to the Father in colourful, imaginative ways. A. W. Tozer puts it best:

> If the Holy Spirit should come again upon us as in earlier times, visiting church congregations with the sweet but fiery breath of Pentecost, we would be greater Christians and holier souls. Beyond that, we would also be greater poets and greater artists and greater lovers of God and His universe.[2]

Let us never give up the adventurous pursuit of creativity in worship.

Insights

RELATIONAL
ACCOUNTABILITY

CHARLIE HALL

As you are learning to lead worship, give yourself to relational accountability. Let your leaders and friends bare their hearts to you about your life and the way you lead worship. Humbly submit and don't detest their honesty. The psalmist David could even submit and learn from a demonized king (see 1 Sam. 17:10-14). Submission and relationship will sharpen you and open your heart for God's purposes.

PSALM 16

Glory: It's What You're Talking About

L O U I E   G I G L I O

Nobody likes exams. They stress us out and make us cram in an attempt to pass them, leaving us anxiously awaiting the hoped for results and causing us to pray like crazy all the while. Tests freak us out because they do not lie. They are measurable, objective, clear-cut, black-and-white evaluations of where we stand on any given issue—their score an undeniable picture of what's true about you and me for all to see.

There's a test for glory, too. You know, "glory"—that buzzword that seems to be floating freely through the ranks of believers these days, effortlessly rolling off our lips in phrases like, "I just want my life to count for the glory of God!" Sounds great, but how do we know if it's true? How do we (and those around us) know what we truly glory in?

Simple. Glory for each of us is what we're talking about. Yep, we know what is supreme in our souls by what comes out of our mouths. Our accumulated words in everyday conversation are the true test of our devotion and affection. In other words, what we talk about most is what we value highest in our hearts.

It's one thing to say, "God, be glorified in me," but at some point we have to honestly break this spiritual phrase into practical, measurable terms. And to do that we must ask the question, "What am I talking about most?" Because, whatever we're talking about most is what we are amplifying (glorifying) with our lives. Think about the massive amount of glory we give to sports teams, pop stars, ourselves, brands of clothing, other people, possessions, experiences and events, as they fill our mouths and dominate our conversations. We are walking, talking billboards all day long, exporting the praises of something or somebody.

Having been made in God's image, we house mirrored souls designed to reflect His glory. By design, we are created to worship (reflect) Him. And though we have fallen from His glory, our sin hasn't stopped us from reflecting worship, value and glory that was intended for Him. We are destined to worship, and that's what we're going to do, constantly declaring the praise of whatever rivets the attention of our hearts.

Imagine carrying a huge mirror everywhere you go. Like it or not, that mirror is going to continually reflect something for all to see. It's going to reflect whatever you hold it towards, whatever it faces. If you turn it away from yourself, it will reflect the objects or people in your path. Facing you, the mirror will reflect your image back to you and others.

It's no different with our souls. They reflect whatever we point them towards. But since we cannot see the soul, how do we know what our soul is reflecting to the world around us? We know by what comes out of our mouths. The truth is, we talk most about what we are impressed by and enthralled with—what our hearts are filled with and fixed on.

That's what's so powerful about the declaration David makes in Psalm 16:8 when he says, "I have set the Lord always [continually] before me; because He is at my right hand, I will not be shaken." The Scripture tells us that David was "a man after God's own heart" (1 Sam. 13:14), and we know that's true because of his actions and words. All throughout his life, in good times as well as in difficult places, David keeps on telling the greatness of God. In all kinds of circumstances he always ends up glorifying God.

But how is it possible to constantly praise God no matter what the situation? We find the answer in verse eight where we see that David was always setting the Lord before him. David knew the secret of aiming his gaze (his thoughts and affections) towards God at all times. The result—God's praise (His glory) is always coming out of his mouth.

In Psalm 16, David declares:

Apart from You I have no good thing (v. 2).

You fill me with joy (v. 11).

I love being in Your presence (v. 11).

My pleasure is being with You (v. 11).

You are my refuge (v. 1).

Once David's heart (mirror) is pointed towards God, amazing things happen. For one, his heart is glad, because aiming our hearts towards an unshakable God brings "inside" joy in any situation. Second, his tongue rejoices. His mouth makes noise. There it is—his tongue (interestingly, some versions read "glory"), or the core of who he is, echoes God's praise. And lastly, to top it all off, his body rests securely as his internal shift of focus influences every pore of his flesh.

So what are you talking most about? Is it the songs? Or music? New gear? Your ministry? The hottest band? The latest conference or CD? What so-and-so said about whatever, or what book you've just read? What you watched on TV last night? Or, somewhere in the midst of it all are you talking about Jesus? Is His name often on your lips as you hang out with friends over a Starbucks coffee or lunch? The degree to which Jesus is the centre of our off-stage conversations is the true test of how much we really have found our delight in Him. Obviously, there's nothing wrong with enjoying and celebrating the stuff of life, but when Jesus' name is rarely found in our words, the test results are clear.

The life that glorifies God is not easy, but it's not complicated either. Such a life begins with little intentional steps as we moment by moment turn our attention to the living, loving Lord of all, allowing His face to prompt our words and satisfy our souls.

INTENTIONAL RELATIONSHIP

DAVID CROWDER

When we look at the Gospels and the letters of Paul, and we see glimpses into the Early Church culture, we see a picture of purposeful life lived in intentional relationship and pursuing Christ-likeness. I am part of a band, which offers an opportunity to embody and model this kind of living, despite the stark difference between the current culture we live in and that which we see modelled within the New Testament Church. These days, from the moment we are born, we breathe in and breathe out an unhealthy sense of individuality; a "pull yourself up by your boot-straps" mentality that defines the individual as responsible only for himself or herself. In a band, you have a rare opportunity to be intentionally vulnerable and open with each other, pursuing Christlikeness. A band by its very nature requires that there be a dismantling of the individual, a coming together for a common goal. This should be recognized and used to propel us further towards the realization of the Kingdom of God.

UNDERSTANDING WORSHIP IN THE NEW TESTAMENT

(Part 2)

CHRIS JACK

In teaching about worship, I often get groups to imagine they are one of the earliest gatherings of Christians and suggest what their worship might have looked like. It's an illuminating exercise. Usually a whole range of ingredients is proposed. Some of these ideas can be explicitly substantiated from the New Testament. Others may only be inferred, with varying degrees of probability. Yet others are more a reflection of people's own practices or those established within Christian tradition. The truth is that the New Testament has relatively little to say in this area. Yes, it contains direction as to how we should worship. But this guidance has much more to do with the heart of worship than with the specific forms it should take. Significantly, we do not have a single description of a service of worship in the entire New Testament! Granted, there are a few passages that discuss aspects of such services (see 1 Cor. 11; 14), but nowhere do we find an order of service or a description of a complete service.

So what shape did their worship take? What were their structures? Or, indeed, were there any? Where were the announcements slotted: at the beginning, in the middle, or at the end? Or did they simply photocopy them and not have a slot for them at all? My example is flippant, but the point is serious. The bottom line is that we do not have sufficient data to allow us to reconstruct a worship service from New Testament times. Moreover, any information we do have points towards a certain amount of diversity of practice within the Early Church, and not a rigid uniformity. In other words, there is no set pattern.

Why is it, we might inquire, that God has not made things more clear for us? Wouldn't it have been better to have a fixed pattern for all to follow? Wouldn't that have eliminated so much of the unholy squabbling and infighting that too often goes on in churches over how we should worship? Why has God not given us fixed patterns? May I suggest that first it is because He has given us something far superior—His Spirit! So Jesus said that we must worship God in spirit and in truth (see John 4:24; see also the teaching of Paul in relation to the Spirit's role in worship in 1 Cor. 12–14).

Second, changing times and circumstances call for changing practicalities. We find evidence of this within the New Testament itself. In the book of Acts, the church in Jerusalem decided to pool their material resources and live as a kind of extended family (see Acts 4–5). However, there is no mention of any other church doing this, either in Acts or elsewhere in the New Testament.

At the same time, worship is not a free-for-all. Although we have neither precise patterns nor a fixed order of service, the New Testament does contain numerous passages that flag, either explicitly or implicitly, various ingredients of the corporate worship of the early Christians:

- Prayer (see Acts 2:42; 1 Tim. 2:1; 1 Cor. 11:4f.; 14:16; 1 Thess. 5:17; 1 Tim. 2:1-3)
- Reading of Scripture (see 1 Tim. 4:13; 1 Thess. 5:27; 2 Thess. 3:14; Col. 4:15-16; 2 Pet. 3:15-16)

- Preaching (see Acts 2:42; 6:2; Eph. 2:20; 1 Cor. 15:1-8; 2 Tim. 1:13f.)
- Table fellowship (see Acts 2:42; 20:7, cf. vv. 20, 25, 28)
- Singing (see Eph. 5:19; Col. 3:15f; 1 Cor. 14:15, 26; cf. 1 Tim. 3:16; Rev. 5:9-13; 11:17f.; 15:3-4)
- Giving to the poor (see 2 Cor. 9:11-15; Phil. 4:16-18; Heb. 13:16)
- Taking up a collection/offering (see 1 Cor. 16:2)
- Public confession of faith (see 1 Tim. 6:12; 1 Pet. 3:21; Heb. 13:15; cf. 1 Cor. 15:1-3)
- Receiving God's blessing (see 2 Cor. 13:14; Luke 24:50)
- The holy kiss of greeting (see Rom. 16:16; 1 Cor. 16:20; 2 Cor. 13:12; 1 Thess. 5:26; 1 Pet. 5:14)
- Response of "Amen" (1 Cor. 14:16; Rev. 5:14; cf. Rom. 1:25; 9:5; Eph. 3:21, etc.)
- Lord's Supper/Communion/Eucharist (see Acts 2:42; 20:7, 11; 1 Cor. 11:2-26)
- Confession (see 1 Pet. 3:21)
- Giving thanks (see 1 Cor. 11:24; Col. 3:17)
- Use of spiritual gifts (see 1 Cor. 14)

Many questions remain unanswered as to how these elements functioned within worship in terms of frequency, order and timing. As Arthur Patzia puts it:

> The challenge of writing about worship in the early Church is not unlike the work of a detective gathering pieces of evidence to solve a crime or a person attempting to assemble a complicated jigsaw puzzle.[1]

Imagine how it would be if we had an order of service in the New Testament. There would be no room for flexibility, creativity or spontaneity. May I say reverently that I am quite sure that God knew what He was doing when He ordained that we should not have such a record. It was no mistake!

HEART AND MIND

JACK HAYFORD

In my experience, theological discussions about worship tend to focus on the cerebral, not the visceral—on the mind, not the heart. "True" worship, we are often taught, is more about the mind thinking rightly about God (using theologically correct language and liturgy), rather than the heart's hunger for Him. But the words of our Saviour resound the undeniable call to worship that transcends the intellect: "God is spirit, and those who worship him must worship in spirit and in truth" (John 4:24). We have been inclined to conclude that "mind" is the proper synonym for "spirit" here, but the Bible shows that "heart" is a better candidate. The words "in truth" certainly suggest participation of the intellect in worship, but it is inescapably second place and dependent on the heart's fullest release first.

Yes, human intelligence contributes to worship, but God's Word indicates He is not looking for something brilliant but for something broken: "The sacrifices of God are a broken spirit; a broken and contrite heart, O God, you will not despise" (Ps. 51:17). These exercises of our enlightened minds may deduce God, but only our ignited hearts can delight Him—and in turn experience His desire to delight us!

"YOU'VE GOT MAIL"

PAUL BALOCHE

"You've got mail." Many of us hear those words each day as we log on to the Internet to check our e-mail. The phrase was also popularized by a movie of the same title a few years ago. Remember when the only option to connecting to the World Wide Web was through a phone modem with a tortoiselike connection speed of 14k? Then we expanded to 56k; then to cable, broadband and DSL. Suddenly we could download volumes of information in seconds with the simple click of a mouse. Learning to hear the voice of God occurs in a similar fashion.

The New Testament commands us to "walk in the Spirit" (Gal. 5:16). The apostle Paul speaks of hearing from God and being taught of God (see Gal. 1:12). The Old Testament tells us that our ears will hear a voice behind us saying, "This is the way, walk in it" (Isa. 30:21). And the story of Elijah tells us of the "still, small voice" (1 Kings 19:12, *KJV*) or "gentle whisper" of the Lord.

God is always speaking to us. Our hearts can be likened to a modem, picking up on the subtle impressions and whispers of the Holy Spirit. For many of us, our ability to discern His voice at first is perhaps slow and faint—similar to the 24k modem. But as we persist in hiding His written Word in our hearts, and practising His presence, we cultivate dialogue, developing a more "broadband" type of connection with the Lord. Impressions, insights, dreams and visions all become clearer as we stay "logged on".

Jesus said in John 14:26, "the Counsellor, the Holy Spirit . . . will teach you all things and remind you of everything I have said to you." A few verses later He gives us the secret or "password" to hearing from Him: "Remain in me" (John 15:4). "Remain." What a great word! To paraphrase it, "Stay online 24/7." In practice, this means cultivating an intentional preoccupation with Jesus as we live our lives and go about our daily schedule.

In Luke 10:38, Martha invites Jesus and His disciples into her home. While Martha is distracted with much serving, her sister, Mary, sits at the Lord's feet, listening to His teaching. Martha complains to Jesus, "Lord, do you not care that my sister has left me to serve alone? Tell her to help me." But the Lord answers, "Martha, Martha, you are so anxious and troubled about many things; one thing is needful. Mary has chosen the good portion, which shall not be taken away from her" (vv. 40-42, *RSV*).

Figuratively speaking, Martha seems to represent the busy, active, extroverted side of our personality, and Mary the receptive, introverted side. This passage highlights our tendency to emphasize "action and doing" over and above "being and listening". Jesus says that Mary has chosen the "good portion", emphasizing that nothing, not even hospitality and service, is more important than a readiness to be still and know Him.

Unfortunately, it's all too easy to be distracted by the demands of our culture—especially a culture that projects goals, action and results as its highest values. Even our churches fall prey to this mentality, and we're driven to respond to every need that arises. Many times "the good" becomes the enemy of "the best".

Let's be reminded once again to carve out time in our lives to simply sit at His feet. And as we go about our daily routines, let's stay logged on to the Holy Spirit, progressively learning to be led by Him through the adventures of this life. Psalm 95:7-8 declares, "Today if you hear his voice, harden not your hearts."

You've got mail!

HEALTHY SOUND-CHECKS

ANDREW PHILIP

Sound-checks and rehearsals can be very interesting times. They sit somewhere between "all of life is worship" and "now let's have a time of worship" and are the first place to look if you want to know whether a worship band really functions as a team.

As musicians, are we doing what will most facilitate others—at this stage the rest of the band and the sound technicians—to prepare for our gathered worship? Or are we focused on self-expression, "getting my sound" and releasing the musical energy that's been bottled up all week?

Try sometimes to start from a place of rest, perhaps even gathering to pray together before setting up equipment. And then think of the sound-check and rehearsal as times of silence broken by necessary sounds—rather than as times of chaotic noise occasionally wrestled into focus.

WORSHIP-LEADING ESSENTIALS

(Part 5) The Powerful Insights of the Prophetic

M ATT R EDMAN

The third chapter of Philippians tells us that we "worship by the Spirit of God" (v. 3). In fact, you can't worship any other way. And so, too, some of the most meaningful and powerful times of congregational worship occur when we set our hearts on course to follow the promptings of the Holy Spirit. He will lead us on adventurous journeys of prophetic worship.

What exactly is prophetic worship? It is not simply spontaneous worship—though it may involve spontaneity at times. The key word in prophetic worship is "insight". To minister in any degree of power and freshness, we must first receive insight from God. This was the key to the perfect ministry of Jesus as He walked the earth in human flesh. He saw what the Father was doing, and did it:

> I tell you the truth, the Son can do nothing by himself; he can do only what he see his Father doing (John 5:19).

When we receive insight, we begin to lead worship with a sense of direction. It's so easy to become all "mystical" about worship leading—believing that anything really spiritual has to be an impulsive, unstructured, spur-of-the-moment thing. But this is not true at all. Sometimes the prophetic and the spontaneous go hand in hand, yet whether we hear the whispers of the Holy Spirit before or during a worship gathering, the key is always insight. We ask the Spirit of God to show us where and how He is leading, and we seek to follow. Sensitivity to the Holy Spirit is the key to breaking fresh ground as a worshipping church.

The scary side is that we never really know whether the little idea that popped into our head was God's prompting or not—until we deliver it. It's like tight-rope walking—once you step out, it's hard to turn back, and the golden rule becomes "Don't look down!"

In other words, once you've launched out into the prophetic, keep your eyes fixed on Jesus. At times I've sensed God prompting me to do something a little unusual (for example, starting off the worship with a time of extended silence, or singing out a particular repetitive line), and we've seen a breakthrough. But I've had plenty of other times when I've ventured out and pretty soon realized that my little idea didn't come from heaven—but from a bad curry I ate the night before. These times are embarrassing, but they also help us to learn and grow.

We soon realize that in our quest for the prophetic benefit of foresight—we also must not neglect the benefit of hindsight. Learning from previous successes and failures is essential for every worship leader who desires to grow in this area. Over time we discover an approach and a pace that is likely to be received well by our congregation—and ways therefore that we might lead the people more effectively and servant-heartedly. The best of these times are a mixture of "Holy Spirit led" and "use your (God-given) head".

Songwriting is also an important element in prophetic worship. As writers of congregational songs, we can seek to reflect the many different seasons of church life. The song "The Heart of Worship" is a personal example of this. As a congregation, we had lost something of our focus in gathered worship, with too much attention on outward things and not enough focus on the heart of our offerings. So for a season, the pastor, Mike Pilavachi, was prompted to take away the sound system, the band and all other outward props so that we might rediscover the heart of what it really means to worship in spirit and truth together. The song simply described and gave voice to what God was doing in us:

> When the music fades, all is
>   stripped way,
> And I simply come;
> Longing just to bring something
>   that's of worth
> That will bless Your heart . . .
> I'm coming back to the heart of
>   worship,
> And it's all about You,
> All about You, Jesus.[1]

In His grace, God had entrusted us with a little song for the moment. Looking back on this season reminds me of just how important a part songwriting can play in prophetic worship.

In summary, the prophetic lead worshipper is on a journey—always asking God for insight as to how to take the next step onward. Prophetic insight is a key that time after time unlocks inspired congregational worship.

Insights

LEADING BOLDLY BUT HUMBLY

CHRIS TOMLIN

The question usually goes something like this: "How do you get the balance between too much performance and being almost non-existent while leading?" This is a very good question. Too much attention to either side of the scale can be a bad use of leadership.

The best leaders understand and know how to live in this tension. There are some leaders who think that they'll just stand there with eyes closed and worship the Lord themselves, and not worry too much if anyone else is. But we have a responsibility to actually *lead* the people God has put in front of us. On the other extreme, we don't want to be a lounge-act performance either. We've all seen those who seem more concerned that people look at them than the Lord. This grieves the Spirit of God and causes the congregation to rely more on someone's personality than the Infinite Providence.

So where does this leave us? It leaves us with balancing *both* aspects: to have the presence (I like that word better than "performance") to call or rally people together to worship our Lord, and also to have the humility to move out of the way and point them to Jesus. Like most things, this ability comes with maturity. It helps if we remember our role as lead worshippers. Put simply, we are worshippers just like everyone else in the room—and for this time and space, God has allowed us the honour and privilege of helping to lead His people.

PSALMING: BECOMING FLUENT IN THE LANGUAGE OF WORSHIP

J. D. WALT

Have you found your worshipping and praying voice in the Psalms? The Bible is made up of 66 books. For the most part, 65 of those books speak *to* us. Fourth-century Bishop and Egyptian theologian, Athanasius, said the Psalms speak *for* us.[1] The Psalms are not the prayers of nice church people. They are the heartfelt, gut-wrenching cries of people like us. The Psalms contain the full range of human emotion and feeling. From the mountain-top of gratefulness, "Give thanks to the Lord, for He is good. His love endures forever" (Ps. 136), to the valley of the shadow of death, "My God, my God, why have you forsaken me?" (Ps. 22), the Psalms exegete the depths of the human heart, mind and soul.

The great Reformation theologian John Calvin said it best when he called the Psalms an "anatomy of all parts of the soul".[2] The Psalms are not on the list of ancillary books for extra credit—they are required reading for passing the class. The Psalms are the praying and worshipping voice of the people of God at all times and in all places.

Perhaps the most significant part of the Psalms may actually be those two small words found just beneath the number and just above the first verse. Those two words are "of David". Seemingly insignificant at first glance, the two words contain the stuff of incarnation; the Word made flesh and dwelling among us. "Of David" shows these lyrical poems are not the poetic musings of philosophical pondering. Quite the opposite is true. The simple words "of David" guarantee these words are the gut-wrenching, heartrending, spirit-lifting cries of a real person with a real life in the real world. Our own storied lives become woven into the Psalms as we insert our name into the blank after "of". The most critical leap for the student of the Psalms comes when those small authenticating words "of David" become "of John" or "of Sarah".

Of the 66 books in the Bible, only the Psalms would speak for us. Christians in all times and all places have learned to pray and to worship with the Psalms. The Psalms give a vocabulary and a voice for faith. They provide syntax and grammar for communicating the depth of our being to the listening, living God. They unearth the full range of the human condition. Whether we are thirsting like a deer for the water brook (see Ps. 42) or burdened under the crushing weight of unconfessed sin (see Ps. 51), we will never learn to worship or pray until we have learned to be honest with ourselves before God.

From depths of despair (see Ps. 69), through long seasons in the waiting room (see Ps. 40), down pathways of self-examination (see Ps. 139) into green pastures of refuge and on through "the valley of the shadow of death" (Ps. 23), the Psalms bring us into touch with our real humanity. Only from here might we reach and touch Divinity.

Pastor, theologian and poet Eugene Peterson offers:

I need a language that is large enough to maintain continuities, supple enough to express nuances across a lifetime that brackets child and adult experiences, and courageous enough to explore all the countries of sin and salvation, mercy and grace, creation and covenant, anxiety and trust, unbelief and faith that comprise the continental human condition. . . . Where will we acquire a language that is adequate for these intensities? Where else but in the Psalms? For men and women who are called to leadership in the community of faith, apprenticeship in the Psalms is not an option; it is a mandate.[3]

May God in His mercy grant us fluency in the Psalms, the language of worship, that we might lead others to follow Him and worthily magnify His holy name. Amen.

SONGWRITING

TIM HUGHES

I write in seasons. I've noticed that there will be times where I feel really inspired. I'll come up with two or three song ideas in a week. Then I could go for months when nothing comes. I've tried to learn to go with these seasons. To make time and space when I feel inspired, and to be sensible when I'm feeling dry.

However, I've also been learning about constantly recording song ideas in a journal. In and out of season, I try to jot down thoughts, quotes and lyrical ideas. Often a theme will be simmering within me, but I don't yet have all the words to express it. It might be months later—sometimes even years—that the whole song comes together. Noting down these themes, and any melodic ideas, has become an essential part of my journey as a songwriter.

A grounded life

WORSHIP: CLEANSING THE CHRISTIAN MIND

DON WILLIAMS

We live in a powerful, symbolic universe. Rationalists believe that concepts determine our lives. But they only have the power to change us when they connect to our imagination. We first imagine what we create. Every building, every scientific model, every painting, every sonata, every piece of prose (including this article) is birthed by an idea fired in our imaginations. Fantasies drive us. We become like what we imagine.

Take, for example, our body image. We imagine how we look and how we would like to look. We exercise, diet, choose flattering or slimming fashion, use the latest cosmetics, freeze our facial muscles—and even go under the plastic surgeon's knife—for social approval, youthful appearance and erotic attraction. We become like what we imagine.

Hugh Heffner, prophet of the sexual revolution, has recreated our symbolic world, not simply out of female nudity, but also out of narcissism and self-gratification in all its forms. His assault is not simply on "Victorian" virtues, but on the whole culture of moral absolutes, delayed gratification and a God-centred life. Now with "porn" acceptable in so much of our society, "adult entertainment" is available to all. What early adolescent doesn't want to be an adult? How better, they presume, than to indulge in adult drugs, adult beverages and adult entertainment? Legal restriction makes it all the more alluring. What goes on behind the bedroom door? Warnings on adult websites are violated by one click. Graphic, perverted sex comes unhindered into every wired home that wants it. The result? People's minds become filled with pornographic images and they become like what they imagine.

Likewise, our imaginations are stimulated with the media symbols of power, wealth, success, affluence and luxury. Sexual images connect to all of this. No wonder advertising associates sex with every conceivable product and saleable lifestyle. To consume a certain beer, to use a certain makeup, to wear a certain brand, to attend a certain concert, to play a certain game—all promising to make you more "sexy", more attractive, more desirable, more successful and more valuable. Those who worship at this altar, through their imaginations, become like what they worship.

A LOOK BACK

In the Roman Empire, power and order were the name of the game. The legions defended the frontiers against barbarian invasion, and imperial ideology held diverse populations together. All of this was made sacred in the worship of the "gods", now centred in the Emperor who himself became divine. Wherever a traveller went, he or she was greeted by the symbols of Roman power and divinity, represented in temples, statues, monumental architecture, baths, theatres, sport facilities and a whole lexicon of holidays. These offered powerful visual impressions of Imperial majesty and the glory of pagan religion. The Coliseum brought the power of Rome before a distracted populace in bloody conflict and symbol. As historians have noted, the games were controlled terror. The message? Don't mess with Rome.

This, of course, meant that the Roman imagination was filled with these omnipresent signs of power. Pageant, sacrifice to the gods, triumphs through the streets of major cities and dramas in the theatres all reinforced Rome's divinity.

The coming of the gospel subverted this. Rather than an Empire filled with gods and goddesses, an Emperor worshipped as divine, a landscape populated by spirits demanding sacrifice, Christians proclaimed the one true God. He is uniquely manifested in His only divine Son, Jesus the Messiah—and by the presence and power of His Spirit. This God comes to sweep the Empire clean of all these lesser divinities, now revealed as unclean spirits. Worship is no longer directed to the divinities of Rome, nor towards the Emperor as the incarnation of that divinity. There is only one Lord, Jesus Christ. No wonder Romans saw Christians as atheists. They denounced the gods and goddesses of Rome. They undermined the very theological-ideological basis of Roman power. Christians had to be stamped out. They were revolutionaries and subversives. They were terrorists (to be sure, non-violent ones) against the whole Roman order.

CLEANSING THE CHRISTIAN MIND

When pagans came to Christ, they carried imaginations filled with the symbols and stories of Roman power. Many of these myths were sexually immoral, brutal and unforgiving. The road to sanctification then must include the cleansing of the imagination from these destructive symbols and stories. In other words, pornography had to go. But how? Lust was everywhere—not simply tolerated, but welcomed. The only answer was to replace these old symbols with a new set of symbols. This is exactly what John does in the book of Revelation.

Richard Bauckham writes that John is taken out of this world into heaven itself so that he can see this world differently. He is given God's perspective over it. He notes:

The effect of John's visions . . . is to expand his readers' world, both spatially (into heaven) and temporally (into the eschatological [final] future) . . . to open their world to divine transcendence. The bounds which Roman power and ideology set to the readers' world are broken open and that world is seen as open to the greater purpose of its transcendent Creator and Lord.[1]

John receives a new symbolic world, heaven itself with God enthroned, the Lamb slain and risen, the sevenfold Spirit, the worshipping angels, the 24 elders, and the saints and martyrs victorious over the enemy and his demonic hordes. The sights of heaven are also filled with the sounds of heaven. These are the sounds of worship. The four living creatures (angels) before the throne never stop saying "Holy, holy, holy is the Lord God Almighty, who was, and is, and is to come." They give "glory, honor and thanks to Him who sits on the throne and who lives forever and ever . . ." (Rev. 4:8-9). The 24 elders cast their crowns before the throne and say: "You are worthy, our Lord and God, to receive glory and honor and power, for you created all things . . ." (Rev. 4:11). Moreover, the four living creatures and the 24 elders fall down before the Lamb (in worship) and sing a new song:

> You are worthy to take the scroll [of destiny] . . . because you were slain, and with your blood you purchased men for God from every tribe and language and people and

nation. You have made them to be a kingdom and priests to serve God, and they will
reign on the earth (Rev. 5:9-10).

What John sees in heaven is the reality—of which
Roman power and the worship of the gods is the par-
ody. In other words, Revelation fills the Christian
mind with new symbols, not of the gods and their
myths, but of the one Trinitarian God. His story cli-
maxes, not in the glory of Rome, which will lie in
ruins under divine judgment (like Babylon) but in
the New Jerusalem come down from heaven with
God and the Lamb as its eternal centre. Bauckham
writes that John's visions "create a symbolic world
which readers can enter so fully that it affects them
and changes their perception of the world".[2] He
adds, "The visual power of the book effects a kind of
purging of the Christian imagination, refurbishing it
with alternative visions of how the world will be."[3]

In his devotional classic *The Imitation of Christ*
Thomas á Kempis shows us how necessary this purging is. He focuses on the imagination as the trigger
for sin. Temptation enters the mind as an evil
thought. "Next, a vivid picture: then delight, and urge
to evil, and finally consent."[4] The evil thought is driv-

en by the "vivid picture" of the imagination. Lust, greed and other desires are aroused and sin is the result.

If this is true, then conversely, godliness is also triggered by truth as it engages the imagination. Fill it with the symbols of heaven, fill it with the story of redemption, and fill it with the power of the slain Lamb. Worship explodes and change is effected. George Marsden writes that the preaching of Jonathan Edwards, revivalist, pastor and America's greatest theologian, aimed at the affections, "to bring people beyond a merely theoretical knowledge of spiritual realities. To do so, he wanted them to form 'lively pictures' of the truth in their mind, so they would have to confront them and react affectively toward them."[5] In Edwards's words, people might be affected by Christ's death by forming "a lively idea of Christ hanging upon the cross, and of his blood running from his wounds".[6]

CONCLUSION

But God's answer is also for us to worship Him by filling our minds, our imaginations and fantasies (hearts) with the pictures, symbols and stories of His kingdom. Again Bauckham writes that John intends "to relate to the world in which the readers live in order to reform and to redirect the readers' response to that world".[7] The best of our current worship lyrics do the same. They redirect our response to our broken, narcissistic world. They open heaven, fill our imaginations with its glory and lead us to facedown passion and devotion to the God who reigns there. We become like what we worship—and as we worship the living God, and populate our imaginations with His symbols and story, we will become more like Him.

The Holy Spirit births such worship in our hearts. He regenerates us and transforms us to become conformed to Jesus Himself. As we fill our imaginations—daily, hourly, moment by moment—with Jesus, His earthly ministry, passion, triumph and heavenly glory, we will be changed. Paul tells the Corinthians,

> Now the Lord is the Spirit, and where the Spirit of the Lord is, there is freedom. And we, who with unveiled faces all contemplate the Lord's glory, are being transformed into his likeness with ever-increasing glory, which comes from the Lord, who is the Spirit (2 Cor. 3:17-18).

LOVING GOD

MIKE PILAVACHI

If we are, first of all, lovers of God, people who are devoted to praising and worshipping Him, then our deeds will be powered by the right motives. When we get our priorities right and put the worship of God first, then everything else falls into place. When we put other things first—even other good things, other good, Christian things—then everything falls apart.

It's as simple as that. St Augustine had a good phrase. He said, "Love God and do what you like." By that he meant that when we truly love Him, then we will want to do the things that please Him.

WORSHIP-LEADING ESSENTIALS

(Part 6) The Brave Perseverance of a Visionary

M ATT   R EDMAN

At one time or another, most lead worshippers discover the need for brave perseverance. There may be glorious seasons when week after week the congregation throw themselves into ever more heightened expressions of worship. But for most of us there are also periods of plain old-fashioned perseverance—when things don't flow quite so easily, and a good deal of endurance is called for. For some brave, persevering lead worshippers, that season continues for years—and they cling to their dreams, with only a few occasional glimpses of a brighter way ahead.

It all starts with a vision—a sense that God is leading us on a journey. God imparts a vision, and week by week it burns deep within our hearts. We long to see our church family venture further and deeper in gathered worship. We may be journeying towards a new freedom of expression together. Or we're aiming for a greater degree of spontaneity within the congregation. But wherever we're headed, there will always be a sense of longing. That is part of the entrustment of being a leader. We live in the tension of the "already established" and the "not yet realized". No visionary lead worshipper stays forever content with where they and their church family are at on this journey. Once we've glimpsed the fact that there's more for us to discover as a worshipping community, there will always be that certain sense of longing.

To put it plainly, the very fact you're a worship leader means that you've signed up for some serious frustration! This is the reality of leadership. God plants the vision in our hearts first, and it burns in our hearts until the dream is realized. If everyone received the vision at the same time, there would be no need for a leader. But as lead worshippers, the Holy Spirit allows us a glimpse of the next destination and begins to unfold the route and pace by which He would have the congregation arrive at that place.

Some vision takes years to realize, other vision is achieved within weeks. I once heard a great piece of advice: "Never overestimate what you can achieve in two weeks. Never underestimate what you can achieve in two years."

The interesting thing is, even when you arrive at one destination point, you'll soon find yourself yearning once again to move on as a congregation to an even deeper place. Leadership is a constant process of unfolding vision.

Gerald Coates once told me, "Maturity is living with the actual whilst aiming for the ideal." Immature leaders aim for the ideal, yet along the way they become increasingly resentful about the actual. Or even worse, they become bitter with the people themselves. Anyone who has ever led worship regularly in a local church setting knows the temptation to become angry with the congregation: "Why aren't they worshipping like I do?" or "Don't these miserable people know how important these musical worship times are?" and other such inner monologue. I only know because I've been there. In hard times, the temptation to self-righteousness is immense. It's during these seasons we need reminding that the only reason we see "more" is because we are involved with leading in this area. We must learn to live with the actual, while never giving up on the dream of the ideal.

One key to living with the actual is to find people who will carry the vision with you. If at all possible, don't journey alone. Good leaders build team. Find other people you can enthuse with your vision for musical worship ministry at your church. Begin to pray together, dream together and stand together. Explore ideas of how to take the next step towards your destination. This is an invaluable thing to do. You will help sustain one another through the hard seasons and have each other to celebrate ministry milestones with. No leader who is in it for the long haul should journey alone.

Worship leading is not always an easy task. At times it involves a whole lot of brave perseverance. But perseverance is not a dead-end street. As well as building character in us as leaders, it also becomes the road to some very exciting places in worship. So, build a team, find God's pace for the journey, and at all costs, keep loving the people of God. Those who sow in tears will reap with songs of joy.

UNITY

GEORGE BARNA

A growing obstacle to genuine worship is the rampant individualism that characterizes so much of our society. Not only does the me-first-and-me-only attitude hinder focus on God, but it is also the enemy of unity. In Romans 15:5-6, Paul reminds us that the Church must be united, for it is in the context of our harmony with God and His disciples that true worship occurs.

It is rare to find a congregation defined by true unity and accountability among all the believers. So many churches remain bastions of internal politics, gossip, judgmentalism and relational factions. Certainly, one of the cornerstones of the life-changing worship experienced by the Early Church is revealed in Acts 2:42-47: the constant fellowship, sharing, serving, accountability and resulting worship that distinguished the

Church from the rest of the religious world.

People whose eyes are riveted on themselves cannot focus upon God. How are we helping people to see beyond themselves? What will it take for us to develop a united family of believers whose first and deepest desire is to worship God rather than get their own way?

UNDERSTANDING WORSHIP IN THE NEW TESTAMENT

(Part 3)

CHRIS JACK

There is much that we do not know about how the first Christians conducted their gathered worship. Yet, there are some fascinating clues scattered throughout the New Testament. In particular, there are traces and fragments of liturgical (worship) material. Even this is not without its difficulties, for New Testament scholars are by no means agreed on just what material is liturgical and what is not. Thankfully, our concern is not to present a definitive list of New Testament liturgical material with which all would concur. Our more modest goal is to set out the main passages of the New Testament that are widely accepted as being of a liturgical nature. As we study the broad canvas of the type of worship material handed down to us in the New Testament, it has much to tell us about early Christian worship.

Certain classifications are commonly used for the New Testament liturgical material.

DOXOLOGIES

Doxologies (from the Greek word *doxa*, meaning "radiance", "splendour," "glory") are expressions of praise to God, using particularly exalted forms of language. They were a regular feature of Jewish worship. The early Christians adopted the form, using existing Jewish doxologies where appropriate, but also developing their own. Some doxologies are simple, others are expanded, at times quite fully.

1. *The* berakhah *(eulogy): "Blessed be God".—* This is a common Old Testament expression of worship. It also resembles the Shemoneh Esreh (the Eighteen Benedictions), an element of the synagogue liturgy. (See Rom. 1:25; 9:5; 2 Cor. 1:3ff.; 11:31; Eph. 1:3ff.; 1 Pet. 1:3.)

2. *"To him be glory [and dominion] for ever [and ever]"*—This is a very common formula, while also being structurally less formal than the berakhah. (See Rom. 11:33-36; 16:25-27; Gal. 1:5; Phil. 4:20; Eph. 3:21; 1 Tim. 1:17; 6:16; 2 Tim. 4:18; Heb. 13:21b; 1 Pet. 4:11; 5:11; 2 Pet. 3:18; Jude 24-25; Rev. 1:6; 5:13; 7:12.)

3. *"Worthy are you/is he"*—While not common, this is a form that is rich in the ways it is expanded. (See Rev. 4:11; 5:9,11.)

CREEDS/CONFESSIONS

While there are no formal creeds as such in the New Testament (these were later developments as the Church worked out and established its theology), many scholars find creedal material in the form of fragments of creedal confessions, or confessional statements. At times, though not always, by any means, the presence of such material is indicated by the use of an introductory formula such as "It says . . .".

Some confessions are brief:

Jesus is Lord (Rom. 10:9-10).

Jesus is Lord (1 Cor. 12:3).

Jesus is the Christ (1 John 2:22).

Jesus Christ has come in the flesh (1 John 4:2).

Jesus is the Son of God (1 John 4:15).

Jesus is the Christ (1 John 5:1).

Others are more developed. (See Rom. 1:3-4; 4:24-25; 8:34; 1 Cor. 11:26; 15:3-5; 16:22; Eph. 4:8; 5:14; 1 Tim. 3:16; 2 Tim. 2:11-13; Heb. 1:3; 1 Pet. 3:18-22; Rev. 15:3-4.)

Significantly, the primary focus of this creedal/ confessional material is the saving work of Christ and His lordship.

BENEDICTIONS

These are expressions of wish or desire for a person or group. Common in Jewish worship, they have been described as "wish prayers". In particular, they invoke grace or peace. They are especially common at the beginnings and endings of letters. (See Rom. 1:7;

15:5; 15:13; 15:33; 1 Cor. 1:3; 16:23; 2 Cor. 13:13; Gal. 1:3; 6:18; Phil. 1:2; 4:23; Philem. 3; 25; Eph. 1:2; Col. 1:2; 1 Thess. 1:1; 3:11-13; 2 Thess. 1:11-12; 2:16-17; 3:5; 3:18; Heb. 13:20-21,25; 1 Pet. 1:2; 5:14; 2 Pet. 1:2; 2 John 3; 3 John 15; Jude 2; Rev. 1:4; 22:21.)

Having already considered doxologies, creeds/ confessions and benedictions, we turn our attention now to prayers.

PRAYERS

While there are numerous prayers and references to prayer in the New Testament, from a liturgical perspective the most notable material is in the form of a number of what have been described as "prayer acclamations". These are: *Amen*, *Abba, Father*, and *Maranatha*.

Amen

"Amen" is a Hebrew word with the meaning "certain, true". In the Old Testament it is used some 25 times to affirm or make binding what has been said, particularly in the context of prayer/praise offered to God (see 1 Chron. 16:36; Neh. 8:6; Pss. 41:13; 72:19; 89:52; 106:48) or curses (see Num. 5:22; Deut. 27:15-26; Jer. 11:5).

In time it came to be a fixed liturgical element in Jewish synagogue worship, uttered at the end of doxologies, benedictions and prayers. It was a means of corporate identification with the utterances of a single individual, whether the leader or a member of the congregation. This usage carried over into early Christian worship. "Amen" was of course regularly used by Jesus, not in a liturgical way, but as an emphatic particle with the meaning "truly, I assure you that . . .". Liturgically, it carries the sense of "let it be so". It is used in this way over 20 times in the New Testament (see Rom. 11:36; 16:27; Eph. 3:21; Phil. 4:23; 1 Tim. 1:17; Heb. 13:21; 1 Pet. 5:11; Rev. 1:6-7; 22:20).

Particularly interesting is 1 Corinthians 14:16, which clearly reflects the custom of saying "amen" in response to someone's utterance (in this instance, praise/thanksgiving) addressed to God. This is, then, one point at which we are in direct contact with the very first believers. For whenever we corporately (or individually) utter the word "amen", we are using exactly the same word they used.

Abba, Father

The word "Abba" is another example of a continuity that stretches from the New Testament to today (see Mark 14:36; Rom. 8:15; Gal. 4:6). Now, as then, we at times express the reality of God being our Father by means of the Aramaic word "Abba". It is self-evidently an address to God, echoing the way that Jesus taught His disciples to pray (see the "Our Father" [Matt. 6:9]) and the way He Himself addressed God (see Mark 14:36). Indeed, it is most probably Jesus' own use of "Abba" that led to this Aramaic word continuing to be used even in non-Aramaic-speaking settings. Is this, then, one of the earliest examples of a worship tradition being established? If so, it is a particularly precious one. For, addressing God as "Abba" was, and is, an indicator of the intimate relationship that Christian believers have with Him. What a privilege to call the infinite God of the universe, who is sovereign over all creation, "Abba, Father"! And how wonderful to identify with fellow believers from the first century right down to the present day as we cry out to our heavenly Father, taking up the word Jesus Himself used in addressing Him: "Abba".

Maranatha

This is another Aramaic word, or, more correctly, two words: "marana" and "tha". Found only once in the New Testament (see 1 Cor. 16:22), it is nevertheless quite significant. It means "the Lord is coming" or, more probably, "our Lord, come!".

Some connect "maranatha" with the Lord's Supper, but this idea is contested by others. "Our Lord, come!" is either invoking the Lord's presence as believers remember Him through the bread and the wine, or it is eschatological, looking forward to, and praying for, His return. Either way, as the believers engage in worship, the focus is on Jesus, desiring His presence. And this is expressed by means of yet another liturgical term with its roots firmly in the earliest traditions.

How illuminating these prayer acclamations and liturgical declarations are—each one a fascinating little glimpse into the worship life of the early Christians.

CREATING COMMUNITY

CINDY RETHMEIER

I love the worship community life at our church that has developed over the past several years. A few things have contributed to this, one of which is that before we begin rehearsal for a Sunday service, my band stands in a circle to pray. We talk about the service and the set list, and then we go around the circle to find out how everyone is doing. Often there is someone who has been dealing with stress from work or a family matter, or someone is not feeling well. We then have those people stand in the middle of our circle, and we pray for them before we pray for our rehearsal and the service. Doing this has given us the chance to know each other better and has created a sense of community between us that is precious. It has been well worth the time spent, even when, in theory, we could have used that time for more rehearsal. It connects us with each other and often it stills the storm going on inside of those who have asked for prayer.

WORSHIP-LEADING ESSENTIALS

(Part 7) The Irreplaceable Quality of Humility

MATT REDMAN

One of the ancient Desert Fathers once noted that "Humans need humility and the fear of God, like the breath that issues from their nostrils."[1] And when it comes to being a lead worshipper, the heart standard of humility is just as irreplaceable a quality.

The heart posture of humility recognizes that God alone can do powerful and meaningful things. By His grace we may get involved with such ministry, but we are ever the carriers and never the cause. The humble heart recognizes the difference between entrustment and achievement. Great is the temptation to think that we had something to do with a particularly poignant success in ministry. Dangerous thoughts. Next thing we know, we're praying less, preparing less and generally less dependent. As Darlene Zschech wisely puts it:

> Momentum can be your best friend. It's like the breath of God causing one day to be more valuable and worthwhile than a thousand . . . But you can abuse that momentum if you stop digging for the gold that gave you it in the first place. Momentum can give you a false sense of security . . . "We can do it". . . . But at what cost? Before we know it, we've abused the privilege and lost sight of the higher call.[2]

Sometimes we have an incomplete picture in our minds of what a humble person really looks like. Humility is more than just a meek and mild "Oh no, no—it wasn't me, it was the Lord" response when someone encourages you in your worship leading. False humility is a tempting garment to wear—but even that involves thinking about yourself. At the end of the day, it's simply another cover-up for pride. Humility only truly blossoms when we stop thinking about ourselves altogether and start to fix our gaze elsewhere.

A former United States senator once commented:

Humility is a manner, a viewpoint, an all-encompassing thing. . . . Humility is expressed through actions; . . . it can be demonstrated simply by stopping and listening to someone. Its essence is putting others ahead of yourself. . . . A real test of humility is how you handle criticism. The natural reaction is to throw up an immediate defense, a quick excuse, a spontaneous rebuttal. The humble way to handle criticism is to try to understand the reasons for the criticism, to look for what truth there might be in it.[3]

These great insights from the world of politics are just as poignant for our role of lead worshipper in our churches. Humility isn't just how you carry yourself on a stage in front of people. It's not even what face-shape you pull when they say nice things to you. True humility starts long before we get up to the front of the church, and touches every area of our lives. Do we seek to put others ahead of ourselves?

Do we spend time with individuals, listening and preferring them? Or are we only good with crowds? And how about when someone offers some constructive criticism of how we lead, or of a song we've written? How do we respond in the depths of our hearts? These are all good tests when it comes to the irreplaceable quality of humility.

Humility is picking up litter when no one's looking, just because you want to serve your community. Humility is letting someone else use your idea. And then telling no one it originated with you. Humility is listening to another, even when you yourself have plenty to say. Humility expresses itself in random acts of kindness performed day in and day out, for God's eyes only—invisible acts that only you and God get to witness. These are some of the telltale signs of a humble heart.

At the end of the day, true humility can never be mustered up or learned by striving. It is the heart instinct of someone who has seen the greatness of God. The humble person thinks about God, and because of Him, about others, too. And as C. S. Lewis once wrote, if you meet someone who is truly humble, "he will not be thinking about humility: he will not be thinking of himself at all".[4]

TRAINING UP OTHERS

Eoghan Heaslip

The heart and character of the person being mentored will determine the pace within the leadership experience. You may find worship leaders who are competent—they're good people and have a real relationship with the Lord—but, for example, don't have a deep enough pastoral heart for the people yet—so they get very frustrated with the pace of the congregation.

Don't give people too much too soon—because you may cause them to think they're further on than they actually are. Try to be consistent and there for them, to the point where you're always behind them, believing in what God's put in them.

WORSHIP-LEADING ESSENTIALS

(Part 8) The Kingdom Mind-Set of a Mentor

MATT REDMAN

One of the best expressions of humility is the act of preferring others. And one of the best ways of preferring others is the act of mentoring. To mentor is to invest what has been invested in you into the life of another. True mentoring is never a form of heavy shepherding or controlling. It is a coming alongside to sharpen and strengthen one whom you perceive to have a calling from God.

If we each think back over our personal journeys in worship ministry, we will all find key people who spurred us on along the way. Some from near, some from afar—and on all different levels. Some do it consciously, and some invest in us without even really knowing they're doing it. Sometimes, even just to be around someone who has a depth of understanding or anointing in an area of ministry can itself be enough to move us on and grow us.

I grew up in a church environment where young people were encouraged to step out and grow. As they regularly reminded us as a church, "It's tidy in the graveyard, but messy in the nursery." The point being that sometimes you don't become skilled at something without first being allowed to be bad at it. As a teenager, my youth leader was Mike Pilavachi. He encouraged me to start leading worship in the youth group at church. When things went well, Mike would affirm me and feed back on why he felt it had all flowed positively. When I did badly, Mike was on hand to suggest where I went wrong and how I might do better next time. And whether it was encouragement or constructive criticism, I always knew it was in the context of someone who was "for" me.

One of the key points of feedback is consistency—to lavish encouragement after the good times without ignoring the messier ones. In my case, Mike would week in and week out feed back to me how I'd led worship, no matter how it turned out. Discipling requires specific encouragement and corrective insight delivered with pastoral sensitivity.

Mentoring is not just to help a person assess how they are doing in practical terms. The real foundational stuff is all about character. A good mentor helps you evaluate the state of your heart and exhorts you to reach for higher heart standards. He or she speaks into areas that might otherwise go unchecked—never to condemn, always to cultivate.

If we take a short-term worldview, we will never see beyond our own efforts. But if we adopt a long-term Kingdom mind-set, before long we will run into the issue of mentoring. Too often in Christian ministry we see people going solo—touring hard, building a career and in some cases ministering over quite a wide area. But there is a deeper call than that for each of us. Whether we minister locally or even travel a little bit, what are we depositing in the lives of the people among whom we minister? Just look at the ministry of Jesus. Yes, He met with crowds—in fact, He met with many large crowds of people. Yet at the same time He invested deeply into the lives of the disciples. He taught them, He challenged them, He encouraged them and He rebuked them. He sent them out to learn for themselves, and He reviewed their efforts with them. And that which He invested in the lives of these men became the seed of the Early Church. The strategy was not worked out through doing enough crowds to build a big enough base to launch the Church. The strategy was worked out through investing deeply into the lives of potential leaders who, changed by the Resurrection and set on fire by the Holy Spirit, did likewise in the lives of others and literally changed the world.

We would do well to let this wisdom seep into our mind-set in ministry. The Kingdom of God is not about one or two people "doing the stuff"—it's about going for it in ministry with all we have, all the while seeking to pass on as much as we can to those we see beginning to flourish around us. And in turn, urging them to do the same with others they see being raised up. This is the economy of the Kingdom.

A few years back, I was leading worship for a week at a U.K. conference called "New Wine". I'd actually been attending this gathering for several years, from the age of 15. That first year, the lead worshipper was Andy Park. Watching from afar as he creatively led thousands of people in worship was massively inspiring. But during the course of the week he actually ministered even deeper into my life—finding some time to pray with me and to talk about developing in worship leading. These moments were foundational for me in terms of realizing that God might be calling me to invest more time and energy into growing into a calling as a worship leader.

Fast-forward five years, and I found myself back at New Wine, this time leading the worship. The week seemed to be going well, and quite frankly, I was encouraged. Then, on the last day of the conference, I felt God speak to me. Sitting on my own in a team room, I was physically and emotionally exhausted and trying to grab some space. In that moment I thought back to my meeting with Andy Park back in 1989. And God asked a question of me: "Whose life have you invested in this week in the same way Andy invested in you?" I had no answer. So focused on the crowds and the big meetings, I had neglected the Kingdom call to "pass it on". It was a painful but important lesson learned.

One of the barriers to mentoring is that sometimes it's a whole lot easier just to do the job yourself. Everything can be running smoothly, and to train someone else up and have him or her start leading in the meetings might complicate things and lose some momentum. Two things are wrong with this attitude. First, it's a very short-term view. A long-term wisdom screams out "Train up others before you yourself burn out". Second, it's simply not "Kingdom". The values of the Kingdom of God urge us to pass on that which we've been entrusted with to others. As Jesus Himself put it, to those whom much has been given, much will be required (see Luke 12:48).

Let us pray that God would form in us the Kingdom mind-set of mentoring—it is a worship ministry essential.

BUILDING A TEAM

REUBEN MORGAN

Although creative people seem to be best at being islands, a worship team is a place for creative people to find community. And although it is our creative gifting that brings us together, the more important aspect is community. For it is life lived in community that really allows us to become like Jesus.

We have been called to build the Church, so as we build the worship team, we need to create a place where people's gifts can be developed, where they can find purpose, and where character can be forged. That means we focus on building with what we have and work at empowering the people already in the team. The important thing is not to see all the opportunity out there, but to see that God's main thing is the Church. If we do the small things really well, then maybe we'll get the opportunity for more (which in reality is more small things).

PSALM 2

Worship for the Nations

DON WILLIAMS

The prognosis for the Church in the West is not good. Most congregations are in decline, with aging membership. Over 70 per cent of all teenagers in the United Kingdom have never been inside a church. Cathedrals stand largely empty. In the United States "mainline decline" continues. For example, the Presbyterian Church has lost two-thirds of its Sunday School enrolment over the last 30 years. Like other historic churches, it is no longer able to reproduce itself. New Age religion, the cults, Eastern mysticism and the quest to develop "one's own spirituality" have replaced vital communities of worship: loving Jesus, loving each other and reaching out to those consumed by sensuality, materialism and the idols of our age.

However grim this picture may look in the West, and there are remarkable exceptions, it is just the opposite in the so-called Third World. There the Church is exploding. This has led Philip Jenkins to speak of the coming "Next Christendom",[1] based not in the north but in the south. Huge congregations and vast populations are coming to Christ in sub-Saharan Africa, the Far East, Central and South America. And what is the nature of this faith? It is squarely evangelical in its message, traditional in its morality, Spirit-empowered in its ministry of healing, committed to community and vibrant in its worship. When we survey the Church worldwide, if we can hear it, an anthem of praise is rising to the Lord Jesus Christ—and this is exactly the plan and purpose of God.

Anchored in the Old Testament, Israel was never chosen for herself. Her mission was to be a light to the Gentiles, to restore the true worship of God to the nations. Lost in the Fall, recovered in Christ, the universal claim of the Living God to be loved and served is now extended worldwide. We live in history's most exciting period of world evangelization. For example, after the Communist revolution, the wife of Chairman Mao Tse-tung claimed that Christianity was only a distant memory in China. She was wrong. Today probably 100 million mainland Chinese have come to faith in Christ. The vast majority of them worship in "underground" house churches. The gospel has spread like wildfire through the suffering of Chinese evangelists and simple peasants who have often paid in blood to bring their people to Jesus. All of this is prophesied and promised in Psalm 2.

> Why do the nations conspire and the peoples plot in vain? The kings of the earth take their stand and the rulers gather together against the LORD and against his Anointed One. "Let us break their chains," they say, "and throw off their fetters" (Ps. 2:1-3).

David sees the nations in rebellion against the Living God. They "conspire" (v. 1) and "unite" (v. 2) to break off the chains and fetters (see v. 3) which bind them. Rebellion against God's authority corrupts their hearts. Their action plan is to assault the Living God and His Anointed One, His King. Their thesis is simple: to be submitted to God, to worship Him and to serve Him, is bondage. This declaration of war is their road to freedom. This mirrors the Fall in Genesis 3. We are always tempted to see freedom as freedom from God, not freedom for God. We think we are made to serve ourselves and we, like the nations, rebel. But in truth, we are made for Him.

> The One enthroned in heaven laughs; the Lord scoffs at them. Then he rebukes them in his anger and terrifies them in his wrath, saying, "I have installed my King on Zion, my holy hill" (vv. 4-6).

God's first response to the nations in revolt is to see their absurdity. How can people who are dust stand against the Holy God, the Maker of the cosmos, the Eternal King enthroned in glory? He simply laughs and mocks their actions. But because He has made them for Himself, for worship and for service, His scoffing turns to anger. His wrath is not an irrational, simple emotional outburst. His wrath is based on His moral character. The nations are to serve their Creator. Their Creator is not to serve the nations. But more than scoffing and rebuke, God speaks. And what is His message? That there is a King, a sovereign. Although the nations revolt, God is still in charge. His King, His Messiah, is enthroned

on Zion, the holy hill of His holy city, Jerusalem. And
it is He that reigns, not the nations. They are to worship God's King. His reign is the divine answer to
rebellion and revolt. He terrifies the nations, because
He is the instrument of God's just wrath. As they
assault Zion, they must deal with God's King and
God's kingdom rule.

> I will proclaim the decree of the LORD: He
> said to me, "You are my Son; today I have
> become your Father. Ask of me, and I will
> make the nations your inheritance, the ends
> of the earth your possession. You will rule
> them with an iron scepter; you will dash
> them to pieces like pottery" (vv. 7-9).

The King now speaks. He reveals the divine
decree. God has proclaimed this ruler to be His Son.
They live in the intimacy of their Father-Son relationship. The New Testament sees this as a prophetic reference to Christ. He is God's Son by nature. But He is
also revealed to be the Son of God by His resurrection
from the dead (see Acts 13:33; Rom. 1:4). As the Risen
Lord, He is the Firstborn of the whole re-creation
of all things. He is the Second Adam, the One who

triumphs over sin and death and reverses the effects of the Fall. He is the One who stills the nations' revolt. They are not destined to destruction. They are not simply to be defeated and cast into hell. As the Son asks for them, they become His inheritance (see v. 8). Perhaps this is the ultimate meaning of Jesus' prayer from the cross, "Father, forgive them, for they do not know what they are doing" (Luke 23:34).

Yes, God has His righteous wrath. But His wrath, in Karl Barth's phrase, is His "next to last word".[2] His last word is His word of promise, His word of mercy, His word of grace: "I will make the nations your inheritance, the ends of the earth your possession" (v. 8). The nations and the whole creation will be brought back to the will and purposes of God. They will submit to His King and His kingdom, or they will be destroyed. Either we receive God's "Yes", or we will receive His "No". He will be Lord of all.

> Therefore, you kings, be wise; be warned, you rulers of the earth. Serve the Lord with fear and rejoice with trembling. Kiss the Son, lest he be angry and you be destroyed in your way, for his wrath can flare up in a moment. Blessed are all who take refuge in him (vv. 10-12).

   With their eternal destiny now at stake, the
nations and their rulers are called to surrender. They
must lay down their arms. They must submit to the
King. They have been warned (see v. 10). And what
does it mean to submit to the King? It means to worship. At its heart, worship is surrender. This psalm
calls the nations, through their rulers, to "serve the
Lord (Yahweh) with fear". This includes the surrender of the will and the submission of the heart. In the
Old Testament the verb here is often used in parallel
with the verb "worship". The *New American Standard
Bible* renders this phrase, "Worship the Lord with reverence." Since He is God, the nations are to submit to
Him with awe. He is holy, He is enthroned in majesty,
He is glorious—fall down before Him, facedown.

   David here expresses the double movement of
worship—we are filled with fear and trembling before
God's majesty, and we rejoice and shout for joy
before God's mercy. We bow down in surrender and
we rise up in joy (see v. 11). Furthermore, we kiss the
Son—not His face but His feet. This is our sign of
submission. But it is also our act of devotion. As
Mary poured out her ointment on Jesus' feet (see
John 12:1-11), as the prostitute kissed His feet and
washed them with her tears (see Luke 7:36-50), so the

kings, the nations and our hearts give up their revolt and surrender with a kiss. Judas' kiss of death becomes our kiss of life as we kiss His feet.

The alternatives are stark. We receive God's mercy or His wrath. The unsurrendered, unworshipping heart is the rebellious heart. If we reject the grace of God, all that is left is the wrath of God. But this warning is, again, in this hour of grace, the "next to last word". David ends the psalm with the last word: "Blessed are all who take refuge in him" (v. 12). As John sees in the Revelation:

> Never again will they hunger; never again will they thirst. The sun will not beat upon them, nor any scorching heat. For the Lamb at the centre of the throne will be their shepherd; He will lead them to springs of living water. And God will wipe away ever tear from their eyes (Rev. 7:16-17).

The purpose of world evangelization is to restore true worship. Rebellious hearts become rejoicing hearts. The world is lighting up with worship. Cold, hard, rebellious hearts are receiving the grace of our Lord Jesus Christ. As a result they are recovering their destiny. They are becoming thankful once again. Their gratitude and praise overflows and God receives the glory. He is the point of it all—our evangelism, our church planting, our worship and our lives in surrender to Him. The nations are laying down their arms of revolt and raising their arms in worship—to the glory of God.

THE BIBLICAL ROOTS OF DRUMMING

TERL BRYANT

The Bible drum is the *tof* (Hebrew), which modern translators mostly call a tambourine. The tof is simply, and more accurately, a frame drum—which we still find in all sorts of cultures around the world today. It has no jingles and its name is onomatopoeic, with the word sounding like the noise the drum makes.

The ancient Scriptures give authority for the drummer to strike the drum, or tof, in celebration (see 1 Chron. 13:8), in praise (see Ps. 150:4), in worship (see Ps. 68:25), for prophecy (see 1 Sam. 10:5-6) and in declaration of the Lord's sovereignty (see Isa. 30:32). For thousands of years people have used drums to announce their own coming. In worship, we sound the drums to declare God's coming.

UNDERSTANDING WORSHIP IN THE NEW TESTAMENT

(Part 4)

CHRIS JACK

The hymns and hymnic material of the New Testament is a great treasure as we consider early Christian worship. Both in its quantity and in its substance, this is the richest worship material of all.

There are sufficient references to singing in the New Testament to show that this was a common element of early Christian worship (see 1 Cor. 14:26; Eph. 5:19-20; Col. 3:16; cf. Acts 16:25). Our difficulty, once again, is to know precisely what was going on. What kind of sung material did they use? Jewish? Hellenistic? How often did they sing? Was it a regular feature of their worship, or something more occasional?

And what about accompaniment? What musical instruments, if any, did they use? Indeed, what did their singing sound like? Here, as in other matters concerning the form and structure of early Christian worship, we simply have to profess our ignorance. For, concerning these sorts of details, the New Testament is silent. Furthermore, specialist studies on the Jewish and Hellenistic backgrounds, exploring the nature and use of music in society and in religion, have yielded no firm conclusions.

> Investigation of the music of the early church has drawn on the efforts of liturgical scholars, musicologists and historians, as well as biblical scholars, in attempting to find out what the music of the earliest Christian church consisted of and where it came from. There are still many questions to be answered, and perhaps many questions yet to be asked.[1]

Even the reference to "psalms, hymns, and spiritual songs" in Ephesians 5:19 and Colossians 3:16 is somewhat enigmatic—at least from our standpoint. Some have attempted a threefold distinction: the "psalms" are Old Testament Psalms, or Christian compositions along similar lines; the "hymns" represent carefully worked verse texts; while the "spiritual songs" are spontaneous, ecstatic, sung offerings. However, the foundations for such distinctions are very tenuous, since we simply do not have sufficient evidence. In fact, most scholars take the view that it is not possible to differentiate these three in any rigid way. There are no neat distinctions; rather, there is considerable overlap in the meaning of the words. It should be noted, too, that, grammatically, the adjective "spiritual" can qualify all three nouns. That is, there is no one category that is necessarily more "spiritual" than the others!

The only factor that allows us to designate any passages as hymns at all is the presence of a more poetic or metrical form. It should be observed that where there is a reference to "song" or "sing" in the New Testament, we are not actually told the substance of what was sung. The only exceptions to this are in the book of Revelation (see Rev. 4:8,10-11; 5:9-10; 15:3-4), and in each of these passages the setting is not early Christian worship but the courts of heaven!

In all, over 100 passages have been proposed as possible hymn material. Here are just some of the more significant and widely accepted ones. Take time to read them and to reflect on their content.

Luke 1:46-55
Luke 1:68-79
Luke 2:29-32
John 1:1-18
Ephesians 1:3-14
Philippians 2:6-11
Colossians 1:15-20
Hebrews 1:3
1 Timothy 3:16
1 Peter 3:18-22

A number of these passages have served to inspire subsequent hymn writers and hymns and songs we sing today that use the biblical words, or are based on them. In this way, we join our song with that of first-century believers. They may not recognize (or appreciate!) the music, but the lyrics would be very familiar!

And what about the lyrics? Perhaps the most striking thing is the extent to which they are focused on the person and work of Jesus. The passages above include many of the most outstanding statements about Jesus' person and work in the whole of the New Testament. In particular, they carry a high Christology, to use a bit of theological jargon. That is, in worship, the Church acknowledges Jesus to be who He is—God, the Son—and worships Him. They are hymns that focus on Jesus and God's redeeming work through Him. Of course, New Testament worship is truly Trinitarian. Jesus is not worshipped apart from, or in contrast to, the Father and the Spirit, but together with them. Indeed, rightly understood, to worship one is to worship all three, for they are one.

CONGREGATIONAL WORSHIP AS A JOURNEY

MATT REDMAN

When it comes to preparing for gathered worship, the key is to think *journey*. We want to be on a progression of some kind during any particular meeting. I like to start with some kind of "call to worship" or "announcement" song—something that awakens us to worship and reminds us of the magnitude of what we do in our time together. From then on in, every song is hopefully a step further into the depths of God—an expectation of encounter.

Sometimes there will be a theological theme running throughout—perhaps a sermon topic, or just a sense that God is wanting to highlight one particular area. Often I'll have one song that I feel strongly is going to be a "dwelling place" during the time—a space where we'll linger for a while and immerse ourselves in a theme.

At some point, too, there must be dedication songs that complete the integrity of our worship with obedience—"sending" songs and "surrender" songs.

The little journey we find ourselves on during a particular service is part of the bigger pilgrimage we're on during our weeks, months and years as a church family. Bear this in mind, and think *journey*.

WORSHIP-LEADING ESSENTIALS

(Part 9) The Constant Expectation of the Heavenly

M ATT   R EDMAN

I've been leading worship through music for half of my life now and have experienced the good, the bad and the sleepy of worship meetings. There are times when everything flows well and we journey seamlessly into the courts of God. There are times when the going is a little tougher, but in the end we journey somewhere meaningful. And there are a few of those "ground swallow me up" meetings where nothing seems to go as planned.

And then there are those other occasions when something far deeper and brighter happens—a breaking through into something distinctly heavenly. Times when every person in the room is overwhelmed by God and overflowing in unstoppable adoration. Times when God's presence moves among us in such a powerful way that every heart is bowed and every tongue stilled. Moments of an intensely intimate reverence as undone hearts encounter the glory of God. And though these heightened times are only occasional, I'm trying to get up to lead worship every time with a constant expectation of the heavenly.

I'm writing this piece two days after one of those moments. Forty-eight hours ago, I was in a packed room in Atlanta at the Facedown songwriters' gathering. On the second night of the gathering, as we worshipped our hearts out through music, something happened. It was an otherly moment—a heightened sense of the glory and grace of God. As we journeyed deeper through spontaneous singing and prayer, there was a very real sense of adventuring spontaneously, yet as one, in the power of the Holy Spirit before the throne of God. For me it was one of those meetings you dream for as a lead worshipper—and once you have such an encounter, there's no going back. It's a little like surfing a great wave and then waiting for the next big one to come. You're hesitant to leave the water until you encounter more of the same. In a sense, all you can do is wait expectantly, knowing there is nothing you can do to conjure up such a moment. The only thing within your power to do is to wait—and make yourself ready to flow with the next big wave that arrives.

Every time we lead congregational worship, we must do so with a longing for heavenly and holy moments and a knowledge that no amount of striving or experience could ever make these moments happen. They cannot be manufactured or formularized. They are grace, pure grace. The only thing we can do is prepare our hearts and create an environment of dependence. As Oswald Chambers said:

> Complete weakness and dependence will always be the occasion for the Spirit of God to manifest His power.[1]

Sometimes our sense of expectancy can be dampened by seasons of dryness. In these seasons it can be so easy to give up seeking God for breakthroughs. The temptation is to settle, especially if we've had years of much perseverance and little progress. I have a deep respect for all those who lead week in, week out in a local church setting and never give up on the quest for freshness and deep encounters with God.

From my experience, a conference is a totally different animal—anyone can be fresh at a conference—there's more expectancy in the air, it's a one-off event, and you can link all of your strongest songs together, without the same risk of having overplayed them. But the Sunday morning service is a whole different thing. Reality kicks in as week by week we live with the actual and aim for the ideal. Leadership in such an environment requires eyes of faith and feet of endurance. We must not allow ourselves to become depressed or discouraged by these seasons. Instead we lean on the sovereign plans of God and learn to ride out, even embrace, these times, all the time crying out for sacred congregational moments in the Lord's presence.

One of the most healthy things to instil in the hearts of a congregation is a sense of readiness. In all too many worship meetings we are simply not "ready". We have not come prepared for an encounter. We are ready and expectant perhaps simply for the natural and social aspects of meeting with other people. But we have not come ready and expectant to meet with the Living God. The key to a constant expectation of the heavenly is to remember that worship is a spiritual thing. In the most powerful and profound worship meetings, "deep calls to deep". It is a spiritual event—the deep places in us responding to and resonating with the deep places of God. As the book of 1 Corinthians 2 informs us, the Spirit searches all things, even the deep things of God (see v. 10). Our prayer should become, "Holy Spirit of God, You are the ultimate Worship Leader. Usher us today into the depths of God." This prayer and posture is a worship-leading essential—a constant expectation of the heavenly.

9 TO 5 OR 24/7?

ROBIN MARK

Fifteen years ago, God led me to a decision that changed my life. No, it wasn't to go into full-time music ministry, nor to sign a record deal with a major distributor, nor anything one would consider remotely "churchy" or music ministry oriented. It was to start a business as a self-employed noise and acoustic consultant!

I felt as strong a call as I had ever had that this was what God wanted me to do. I gave up my salaried post as a college teacher and, with a wife and child, an overdraft, some borrowed cash (actually from my pastor), and a tiny little start-up grant from my local enterprise organization, I launched myself upon an unsuspecting noisy world! F. R. Mark and Associates, "Noise and Acoustic Consultants", was born. I rented an office for £10 per week in a town outside Belfast, bought an Amstrad computer and a telephone, and went for it.

Now, was this call any less in God's eyes than a call to full-time worship ministry? Was the Father's hand set more lightly upon this venture than it would have been upon a church-based career? Was this just a passing diversion before God really blessed me with enough royalty income to spend glorious day after day reclining on a leather sofa in the music room, creating heavenly melodies in splendid isolation from the rotten old world? Actually . . . no.

In our society, we separate the sacred and the secular as if one had a higher calling than the other. It was never so in the Hebrew mind-set. The apostle Paul went out of his way to talk about all the different parts of the body and how one part should not think itself superior to another (see 1 Cor. 12). Whatever our hand finds to do, we should do it with all our might, as unto the Lord (see Eccles. 9:10). In other words, your work can be an act of worship, just as distinctive and important as the finest song that will ever be written.

In the fullness of time, God has resourced out some of the songs of worship I've composed and I now receive some financial reward for this creativity.

I am truly blessed and thankful for His grace in this area. But more than that, being self-employed meant I was able to go to conferences, concert tours, visit churches all over the world and fund some of my early recordings, without needing to ask my employer for days off! (Unless I was talking to myself at the time.) Having that income meant I didn't have to strain to produce another song, trying desperately to maintain my highest motivation, while knowing that I needed the income from the song to survive.

Now, don't get me wrong. I truly admire the full-time worship leaders and musicians that have blessed us all over the years. I know worship leaders who've re-mortgaged homes and sacrificed income to bring God's people together in worship—men and women who ministered so graciously in the early years of the worship renewal, visiting Northern Ireland from England, for little more than petrol money and a kind word. These were men and women of faith who heard the call to step out into full-time worship ministry when there wasn't any real support or assistance.

But one thing is sure. If you ask these guys what motivated their decision, they will surely tell you that it wasn't the need for success or the desire to be in full-time service (we're all in full-time service, by the way). Nor was it money or recognition or even just the kudos that comes with being part of music stuff. No, not at all. It was God's call—no different from my call to business. The same call as the shop worker, the taxi driver, the business manager, the nurse or the doctor.

God has to be careful with us. We are so slow to learn—at least I am. I know now, looking back, that my natural attitude would have been to run before I could walk, that I would have got totally caught up in something that wasn't for me and blown everything, that I needed to be a noise consultant. (Honest!) He knows what each of us needs to be and where we need to be.

So, here's the thing. Don't strive to be in full-time music ministry. That is a calling that demands great sacrifice and great commitment. Don't strive to become a full-time musician just because it seems the appropriate or cool thing to do. For sure, if the call on your life seems so strong and real, then, if the door opens, go for it. But don't expect it to be any different from any other work. There are great disappointments and challenges on that walk. It has to be a call. It must be a call. And it can be a call to work in the supermarket, to feed your family and to play your songs of worship in your spare time. That's as high a call as anyone's, if it's what God calls you to do.

And what of my business? Well, God has truly blessed me. I have clients across the whole spectrum of business life in Ireland, including pub and club owners, entertainment companies, government and industry. I have met hundreds upon hundreds of ordinary people that I otherwise would never have known. Some of my songs have been motivated and formed around these relationships. And I earn some money! I have three full-time employees and a couple of part-timers. I now have been graced to take on the role of director of worship in my home church and work a wonderful one day a week there. Maybe one day soon I'll hear the call to go full time. Maybe the business will decline! Maybe I'll need to find work elsewhere. Maybe I'll never hear the full-time music ministry call. All I know is that His ways and His thoughts are higher than ours, and that He knows the plans He has for us.

Listen for the call, and no matter how strange it might seem, go where He calls you to go. Work the 9 to 5, but worship 24/7!

WORSHIP-LEADING ESSENTIALS

(Part 10) The Biblical Perspective of the Big Picture

M A T T   R E D M A N

Sometimes in worship we think too small. Not that we should be dreaming of leading before thousands. Absolutely not. Rather, we should be realizing that, in reality, we join with millions and millions. Yes, so often we think far too small and miss out on the incredible truth of what is really occurring. Every single time we gather to worship God, we don't just join with a choir of tens or hundreds. We accompany the whole host of heaven, the song of all creation, and the choir of the redeemed who lift up an anthem to the Almighty throughout the nations.

One of the biggest obstacles to consistently fervent worship in a local church is that we miss the magnitude of the occasion. We focus on the four walls surrounding us, and that becomes our reality. We see and hear a group of people in or out of tune with each other—sometimes passionate, at other times a little apathetic. And that becomes our whole reality. But there is a bigger picture to be seen.

Most of us have found ourselves in the midst of a large crowd at some event or other. Whether it's 1,000 or 100,000 people, we experience an amazing dynamic when we're part of that many gathered voices. As I write this, I have just had the privilege of being involved in a wonderful worship event in Belfast, Northern Ireland. It was inspiring to see over 7,000 Christians from many streams of the Church gathering together in the heart of the city, unified around the throne of God in worship. At times we sang unaccompanied—and believe me, the sound of 7,000 Irish voices in heartfelt praise is an amazing thing. But, for me, the excitement felt on such occasions goes way beyond the natural dynamic of lots of people under one roof singing their hearts out—as special and powerful as that can be. To me, the profound nature of such a gathering is heightened when we realize that, as beautiful a sound as it is, it is still just the faintest whisper. Just a tiny foretaste of the true reality of all that is and is to come. There is a louder shout and a sweeter song to be heard. As the old hymn says, "Hark how the heavenly anthem drowns all music but its own."[1]

The Belfast gathering left a big impression on me—but, of course, it's not every day we get to join with such grandiose choirs in worship. And, let's be honest, singing our hearts out in a home group setting with three or four of our less vocally talented friends just isn't the same somehow. Or is it? Perhaps it can be, if we somehow in our spirits grasp the bigger picture. However small or large a gathering, however in or out of tune we are musically, we are joining with the eternal flow of praise that rises every moment before the throne of God. Short of God's own voice, it is the greatest sound in all history.

Take a moment to put the sound of this worshipping choir into perspective. Imagine every language you've ever heard. Every accent and dialect. Every beautiful vocal sound. Add to that every harmony and every crowd, every choir, every large gathering. As these voices blend into one in your imagination, they are just the tiniest ripple of what is to come. One day every tribe and tongue will join this song. Multitudes and multitudes of passionate worshippers. Add now the sounds of all creation, every birdsong you ever awoke to, every ocean wave you heard reach shore, every clap of thunder, every whistling of the wind, every wild animal roar—"Then I heard every creature in heaven and on earth, and under the earth, and in the sea, and all that is in them singing" (Rev. 5:13)—blend this sound with those cries of the nations, and the orchestration begins to take shape. Yet it is still a mere whisper. Even in our wildest imaginations we still hear merely in part. Now come the melodies and harmonies of the heavens—10,000 times 10,000 angels in joyful assembly, and those strange living creatures speaking ceaseless praise.

This is the big picture—the true biblical perspective of what worship really looks like and will look like before the heavenly throne. As lead worshippers, we must somehow hear beyond the sounds and harmonies flowing within the four walls of the building we use for church gatherings and attune our hearts to this grand eternal flow of praise. And then somehow, in the power of the Holy Spirit, lead our people into the same revelation. This is a worship-leading essential—a biblical perspective of the big picture in worship that will help us more than we could ever imagine.

ENDNOTES

Worship-Leading Essentials (Part 2)
1. Kevin Navarro, *The Complete Worship Leader* (Grand Rapids, MI: Baker Books, 2001), p. 17.
2. Marva J. Dawn, *A Royal Waste of Time* (Grand Rapids, MI: Eerdmans Publishing, 1999), p. 68.
3. Carol Wimber, *John Wimber: His Influence and Legacy,* ed. David Pytches (Surrey, England: Eagle Publishing, 1998), n.p.
4. Edmond Budry, "Thine Be the Glory", 1884, quoted at *The Cyber Hymnal.* http://www.cyberhymnal.org (accessed January 2005).
5. John Piper, *Seeing and Savoring Jesus Christ* (Wheaton, IL: Crossway Books, 2001), n.p.
6. Tim Hughes, "Here I Am to Worship", © 2001 Kingsway's Thankyou Music, 26-28 Lottbridge Drove, Eastbourne, East Sussex, BN23 6NT, England.

When the Tears Fall . . .
1. Dan Allender, "The Hidden Hope in Lament", *Mars Hill Review,* 1 (1994), pp. 25-38.
2. Tim Hughes, "When the Tears Fall", © 2003 Kingsway's Thankyou Music, 26-28 Lottbridge Drove, Eastbourne, East Sussex, BN23 6NT, England.
3. Ibid.
4. Allender, "The Hidden Hope in Lament".
5. Hughes, "When the Tears Fall".

Spiritual Conversations Outside the Sanctuary

1. Christina Rossetti, "In the Bleak Midwinter", 1872, quoted at *The Cyber Hymnal.* http://www.cyberhymnal.org (accessed January 2005).
2. Amy Lee and Ben Moody, "Bring Me to Life", © 2003 Wind-Up Records, 72 Madison Avenue, New York, NY 10016.
3. Barry Taylor, "The Nature of Religion in Contemporary Culture and the Missional Task" (address, the installation of Wilbert Shenk, Chair of Missiology, Fuller Theological Seminary).
4. Amy Lee and Ben Moody, "Bring Me to Life".
5. Walter Brueggemann, foreword to *Psalms of Lament,* by Ann Weems (Louisville, KY: Westminster John Knox Press, 1995), n.p.

Understanding Worship in the New Testament (Part 1)

1. David Peterson, *Engaging with God* (Leicester, England: Apollos, 1992), p. 110.
2. R. P. Martin, *Worship in the Early Church* (London: Marshall, Morgan and Scott, 1974), p. 22.
3. Arthur Patzia, *The Emergence of the Church* (Downers Grove, IL: InterVarsity Press, 2001), p. 186.
4. David Peterson, *Engaging with God*, p. 101.

Worship-Leading Essentials (Part 4)

1. We human beings are made in such a way that our ears can hear around 300,000 different tones, and our eyes distinguish between 8 million colour differences. Thomas Dubay S.M., *The Evidential Power of Beauty: Where Science and Theology Meet* (San Francisco: Ignatius Press, 1999), pp. 230-231.

2. A. W. Tozer, *Whatever Happened to Worship?* (Camp Hill, PA: Christian Publications, 1985), n.p.

Understanding Worship in the New Testament (Part 2)
1. Arthur Patzia, *The Emergence of the Church* (Downers Grove, IL: InterVarsity Press, 2001), p. 183.

Worship-Leading Essentials (Part 5)
1. Matt Redman, "Heart of Worship" © 1997 Kingsway's Thankyou Music, 26-28 Lottbridge Drove, Eastbourne, East Sussex, BN23 6NT, England. All rights reserved.

Psalming: Becoming Fluent in the Language of Worship
1. Eugene Peterson, *Working the Angles: The Shape of Pastoral Ministry* (Grand Rapids, MI: Eerdmans Publishing, 1987), p. 56. In writing this brief essay, I borrowed generously from the thoughts of Eugene Peterson. His book has been a tutorial in my own life of prayer.
2. Ibid., p. 58.
3. Ibid., p. 57.

Worship: Cleansing the Christian Mind
1. Richard Bauckham, *The Theology of the Book of Revelation* (Cambridge, England: Cambridge University Press, 1993), p. 7.
2. Ibid., p. 10.
3. Ibid., p. 17.
4. Thomas á Kempis, *The Imitation of Christ* (London, England: Penguin Books, 1952), n.p.
5. George M. Marsden, *Jonathan Edwards: A Life* (New Haven, CT: Yale University Press, 2003), p. 161.

6. Ibid., p. 162.
7. Bauckham, *The Theology of the Book of Revelation*, p. 20.

Worship-Leading Essentials (Part 7)
1. Anselm Gruen, *Heaven Begins with You: Wisdom from the Desert Fathers* (NY: The Crossroad Publishing Company, 1999), p. 22.
2. Darlene Zschech, "The Power and Pitfalls of Success", *Worship Leader* (January/February 2003), pp. 34-35.
3. Mark Hatfield, interview, "Integrity Under Pressure", *Leadership*, vol. ix, no. 2 (Spring 1988), pp. 128-132.
4. C. S. Lewis, *Mere Christianity* (London: HarperCollins Publishers, 2002), p. 128.

Psalm 2
1. Philip Jenkins, *The Next Christendom: The Coming of Global Christianity* (Oxford, England: Oxford University Press, 2002), n.p.
2. Karl Barth, *The Epistle to the Romans* (London, England: Oxford University Press, 1933), pp. 42, 111.

Understanding Worship in the New Testament (Part 4)
1. Wendy Porter, "Creeds and Hymns, Music", *Dictionary of New Testament Background* (Downers Grove, IL: InterVarsity Press, 2000), p. 712.

Worship-Leading Essentials (Part 9)
1. Oswald Chambers, *My Utmost for His Highest* (Oswald Chambers Publications Association Ltd, 1927), p. 132.

Worship-Leading Essentials (Part 10)

1. Matthew Bridges, "Crown Him with Many Crowns", quoted in *The Celebration Hymnal* (Nashville, TN: Word Music, 1997), p. 45.

Paul Baloche is the writer of songs such as "Open the Eyes of My Heart" and "Above All". Married to Rita, with three children, he is worship pastor at Community Christian Fellowship in Lindale, Texas. He also edits www.leadworship.com.

George Barna lives in Southern California with his wife, Nancy, and their two daughters. He is the directing leader of The Barna Group, Ltd, and the founder of Barna Research Group, a full-time marketing research company located in Ventura, California. BRG has been providing information and analysis regarding cultural trends and the Christian Church since 1984.

Terl Bryant lives in London with his wife, Juliette, and their four children. Founder of the Psalm Drummers vision, Terl has drummed for artists such as Faith Hill, John Paul Jones (ex Led Zeppelin) and Sir Cliff Richard, as well as with lead worshippers such as Matt Redman, Paul Baloche and Graham Kendrick.

Chris Cocksworth is the principal of Ridley Hall, Cambridge, a theological college in the United Kingdom, where he lives with his wife, Charlotte, and their five children. Chris is also a member of the Church of England Liturgical Commission and is currently involved with the compilation of the definitive edition of *Common Worship Daily Prayer.*

David Crowder lives in Waco, Texas, with his wife, Toni. As a young college student, he and a friend started a church for their fellow Baylor University students. Not long after, David felt God calling him to write worship songs that students in his church could relate to, hence the David Crowder Band was born. Their albums include *Can You Hear Us* and *Illuminate.*

Louie Giglio and his wife, Shelley, head up the Passion network—a ministry on college campuses across the United States of America. Together they share a passion to see the glory of God treasured and amplified among this generation of college students.

Charlie Hall and his wife, Kimberlyn, live in Oklahoma, where they serve with Bridgeway Church. Charlie leads worship at many Passion college events and features on all of their live albums. His solo projects with Sixsteps Records include *Porch and Altar* and *On the Road to Beautiful.*

Jack W. Hayford is the founding pastor of The Church On The Way, Van Nuys, California, and is President of the International Church of the Foursquare Gospel. Married to Anna, he is the author of almost three dozen books and has composed over 600 hymns, songs and choruses, including the classic "Majesty".

Eoghan Heaslip lives in Dublin, Ireland, with his wife, Becky, and their two daughters, where he serves as worship pastor for the CORE Church team. He has recently released his second solo album, *Grace in the Wilderness.*

Brian Houston, and his wife, Bobbie, are senior pastors of Hillsong Church in Sydney, Australia, where they live with their three children. Brian is national president of the Assemblies of God in Australia, and was the founder of Australian Christian Churches, an alliance representing approximately 1,200 churches and 200,000 Christians in Australia.

Tim Hughes is married to Rachel and has been leading worship at the Soul Survivor festivals since 1997. He currently leads worship at Soul Survivor events globally and edits www.passionforyour name.com, which offers online teaching, conferences and seminars for lead worshippers. He wrote the widely known song "Here I Am to Worship" as well as a number of other familiar worship songs.

Chris Jack is chaplain and lecturer in Applied Theology at the London School of Theology, where his areas of special interest are John's Gospel and Worship & Spirituality. He is married to Babs, and they have two grown children.

Robin Mark is based in Belfast, Ireland, with his wife, Jacqueline, and their three children. As well as leading worship and writing songs, Robin also heads up a successful business, F. R. Mark and Associates, and lectures in acoustics at Belfast's Queens University. His recordings include the widely known *Revival in Belfast* album.

Reuben Morgan is part of the worship team at Hillsong Church, Sydney, Australia, where he lives with wife, Sarah, and their son, Jones Berlin. Writer of "Lord I Give You My Heart" and many other widely used congregational songs, Reuben has recently released his first solo project *World Through Your Eyes*.

Sally Morgenthaler is the founder of Sacramentis.com and Digital Glass Productions. As a speaker and consultant, her aim is to help many lead worshippers to "re-imagine worship for a new world". Sally is the mother of two children, Peder and Anna.

Nigel Morris lives in Anaheim, California, with his wife, Lynne, where they both serve on the staff of the Vineyard Christian Fellowship. Nigel oversees the worship music department, the compassion ministry and the men's ministry.

Robin Parry lives in Worcester, England, and is commissioning editor for Paternoster. He is also author of *Worshipping Trinity: Coming Back to the Heart of Worship* (Milton Keynes: Paternoster, 2005).

Mike Pilavachi is the senior pastor of Soul Survivor Church in Watford, England, and is a director of Soul Survivor Ministries UK. He has also authored several books, including a book about the subject of worship, *For the Audience of One*.

Andrew Philip moved to the United Kingdom from South Africa five years ago, and works with Matt Redman as musical director and coeditor of Heartofworship.com. Andrew has played keyboard with many different lead worshippers and has produced albums for Soul Survivor, Paul Oakley and Matt Redman.

Todd Proctor is both worship pastor and lead pastor at Rock Harbor Church in Costa Mesa, California. Todd has a heart to write congregational worship songs and has one solo album entitled *Found*. Todd is married to Lisa, and they have three children.

Beth Redman is married to Matt, and they have two children. A former evangelist to school students, and singer with The Worldwide Message Tribe, Beth has written two Soul Sister books, *How to Be a Girl of God* and *The Truth Shall Set You Free,* as well as cowriting with Matt songs such as "Blessed Be Your Name" and "Let My Words be Few". She has a heart to equip and empower young women to make a difference in their generation.

Matt Redman is a lead worshipper and songwriter living in the south of England. His songs include "Heart of Worship" and "Blessed Be Your Name". Matt is also the author of the books *The Unquenchable Worshipper* and *Facedown,* and he edits Heartofworship.com.

Cindy Rethmeier is a lead worshipper and song-writer at the Anaheim Vineyard Church in California. Married to Steve, with two children, Cindy has also sung on many Vineyard USA children's albums such as *Change My Heart, O God* and *Fruit of the Spirit.*

David Ruis, his wife, Anita, and their four children have been involved in pastoral ministry since the mid-1980s, having been regional overseers with the Association of Vineyard Churches in Canada until 2002. David travels internationally, leading worship and speaking, and partnering with church plants in Nepal and Northeast India. Writer of songs such as "Every Move I Make" and "You Are Worthy of My Praise", David now lives in California, and is currently processing his next steps in church planting.

Chris Tomlin is the writer of worship songs such as "Forever", "Famous One" and "How Great Is Our God".

He lives in Austin, Texas, and has recently written the book *The Way I Was Made.*

John David (J. D.) Walt, Jr, is vice president of Community Life and dean of the Chapel at Asbury Theological Seminary, in Asbury, Kentucky. An ordained elder in the Texas Annual Conference of the United Methodist Church, he is cowriter of the song "The Wonderful Cross" with Chris Tomlin. J. D. and his wife, Tiffani, have one son, John David III.

Don Williams is married to Kathryn Anne, and they live in Capistrano Beach, California. He was senior pastor at the Coast Vineyard, San Diego, California, for many years, and has multiple theological degrees. He is the author of many books, including the Psalms volumes of *The Communicators Commentary.*

Darlene Zschech, her husband, Mark, and their three daughters, live in Sydney, Australia. Darlene has been part of the Hillsong Church praise team since 1986, and has led the Worship and Creative Arts Department since 1996. Author of *Extravagant Worship* and writer of "Shout to the Lord" and many other widely used congregational songs, Darlene has also released a solo studio album *Kiss of Heaven.*

The Heart of Worship Files

Compiled by Matt Redman

The Church is in constant pursuit of the 'heart of worship'. Together, we journey on to learn more and more of what it really means to bring meaningful offerings to the heart of God. Thoughts, words, deed, and songs—the whole of our lives as a response to His immeasurable worth.

This book is for all those who find themselves on such a pilgrimage. Lead worshippers, pastors, musicians, dancers, singers—and anyone with a heart to worship. Within these pages you'll find a mixture of creative Bible insights and hands-on advice on how to lead worship and write congregational songs.

survivor

The Unquenchable Worshipper

by Matt Redman

This book is about a kind of worshipper.

Unquenchable. Undivided.
Unpredictable.

On a quest to bring glory and pleasure to God, these worshippers will not allow themselves to be distracted or defeated:

Unstoppable. Undignified.
Undone.

Worshippers who long for their hearts, lives and songs to be the kind of offerings God is looking for.

This is unashamedly a book about God and living a devoted life in His presence. Worship is *about* God, *to* God and *for* God. *The Unquenchable Worshipper* shouts this truth out loud.'

Mike Pilavachi, Soul Survivor

survivor